WHEN PLAGUE STRIKES
THE BLACK DEATH, SMALLPOX, AIDS

OTHER BOOKS BY JAMES CROSS GIBLIN

Be Seated: *A Book About Chairs*

Chimney Sweeps: *Yesterday and Today*

From Hand to Mouth: *Or, How We Invented Knives, Forks,
Spoons, and Chopsticks & the Table Manners To Go With Them*

Let There Be Light: *A Book About Windows*

Milk: *The Fight for Purity*

The Riddle of the Rosetta Stone: *Key to Ancient Egypt*

The Skyscraper Book

The Truth About Santa Claus

The Truth About Unicorns

WHEN PLAGUE STRIKES

STRIKES

THE BLACK DEATH, SMALLPOX, AIDS

BY

JAMES CROSS GIBLIN

WOODCUTS BY
DAVID FRAMPTON

HARPERCOLLINS*PUBLISHERS*

When Plague Strikes
The Black Death, Smallpox, AIDS
Text copyright © 1995 by James Cross Giblin
Illustrations copyright © 1995 by David Frampton
All rights reserved. No part of this book may be used or reproduced in any manner
whatsoever without written permission except in the case of brief quotations embodied
in critical articles and reviews. Printed in the United States of America. For information
address HarperCollins Children's Books, a division of HarperCollins Publishers, 10 East
53rd Street, New York, NY 10022.

Library of Congress Cataloging-in-Publication Data
Giblin, James.
  When plague strikes : the Black Death, smallpox, AIDS / by James Cross
Giblin ; woodcuts by David Frampton.
    p.   cm.
  Includes bibliographical references and index.
  ISBN 0-06-025854-3. — ISBN 0-06-025864-0 (lib bdg)
  [1. Plague—History.   2. Smallpox—History   3. AIDS (Disease)—History.
4. Epidemics—History.   5. Diseases—History.]   I. Frampton, David, ill.
II. Title.
RA644.PZG53   1995   94-39881
614.4'9—dc20   CIP
                                                                       AC

Typography by Al Cetta
1   2   3   4   5   6   7   8   9   10
❖
First Edition

ACKNOWLEDGMENTS

For their help in supplying me with research material and advice, I want to thank the following people and institutions:

Sue Alexander; American Foundation for AIDS Research; Marc Aronson; The Boston Athenaeum; The Cleveland Museum of Art; Russell Freedman; Friends of the Quilt; Gay Men's Health Crisis; God's Love We Deliver; The Huntington Library; Murray Liebman; Davida N. List; Antonia Markiet; The Metropolitan Museum of Art; Jim Murphy; the New York Public Library; Jeanne Prahl; Jane Resh Thomas; and my editor, Barbara Fenton.

Special thanks to Marilyn Souders, Librarian, *Newsweek* magazine, who provided copies of early articles about the AIDS epidemic and later pieces about Rock Hudson, Ryan White, Magic Johnson, and Arthur Ashe.

I also owe a debt of gratitude to Dr. J. W. Hopkins, Department of Biology, Washington University, who read the manuscript from a scientist's point of view and kept me from making some embarrassing mistakes. Any that remain are entirely my responsibility.

—J.C.G

CONTENTS

CONTENTS

AIDS

PROLOGUE

THE PLAGUE OF ATHENS

L ike all epidemic diseases, the Plague of Athens struck suddenly and without warning. It happened early in the summer of 430 B.C., when the city was crowded with refugees from the countryside.

Athens had been at war for almost a year with the neighboring Greek city-state of Sparta, and the refugees had fled to the city to escape the fighting. Surrounded by mountains and protected by strong fortifications, Athens seemed to be a safe haven. Then the disease came, not by land but by sea.

It is thought that infected sailors on a ship from Egypt brought the mysterious illness to Greece. The first cases were reported in Piraeus, the port that served Athens, and from there it quickly spread to the larger city.

Within days hundreds of people fell ill. The first symptoms were a severe headache and redness of the eyes. These were followed by inflammations of the tongue, hoarseness, and a hacking cough. Then came severe intestinal upsets, including vomiting and acute diarrhea. Temperatures rose, and at the fever's height the body broke out all over in reddish spots.

In the disease's later stages, its victims often sank into a delirium. Those who perished usually died between seven and nine days after the appearance of the first symptoms.

Greek physicians had never seen anything like this disease, and they did not know how to treat it. Consequently, the death rate was extremely high. Although no complete records exist, historians estimate that thousands of people—at least a third of the population—died in Athens during the six months the epidemic raged.

Making matters worse were the living conditions of the refugees. Because there were no houses for them, many had sought shelter in makeshift huts. There the bodies of the dying "lay heaped one on top of another, and half-dead creatures could be seen staggering about in the streets." So wrote the Greek historian Thucydides.

Those who survived the disease were often left with terrible scars. Some lost their eyesight, others their memory. Even those who had not been infected suffered from the effects of the epidemic. With so many dead and dying, a cloud of despair and hopelessness descended on Athens. Respect for the law dwindled and crime soared because, as Thucydides wrote, "no one expected to live long enough to be brought to trial and punished."

Besides its impact on the people of Athens, the plague also changed the course of history. In the fall of 430 B.C., the Athenian leader Pericles—thinking the worst was over—sent his navy to capture a Spartan stronghold. But the ships had barely set sail when the disease broke out among the sailors and the fleet was forced to turn back.

The same thing happened to a later expedition led by Pericles himself. A fresh outbreak not only carried off many of his men, but also infected Pericles, who died shortly thereafter. Deprived of its leader and weakened by the plague, Athens struggled on but eventually lost the war with Sparta.

What was the mysterious disease that brought down the great Athenian empire? Modern medical experts can't be sure. Judging from the reported symptoms, some think it was a lethal form of scarlet fever. Others believe it may have been typhus, smallpox, or the bubonic plague. Whatever it was, it must have been a new disease to the unfortunate residents of Athens. Otherwise, it would not have mushroomed into an epidemic.

THE CAUSES OF DISEASE

All infectious diseases—diseases that can be "caught"—are caused by bacteria or viruses. Bacteria are tiny, one-celled organisms that can be seen only under a microscope. Viruses are even smaller. It is difficult to study them in detail even with the most powerful electron microscopes.

All viruses and many bacteria are parasites. This means that they cannot survive on their own but need a plant or animal host in or on which they can find shelter and nourishment. There they reproduce themselves, often with great rapidity.

Many kinds of bacteria are helpful, aiding in such processes as the digestion of food, the decomposition of organic wastes, and the formation of soil. But other types of bacteria, and many viruses, are extremely destructive. They infect their hosts with diseases that may end up killing them.

These dangerous bacteria and viruses enter the human body by various means. Some, like those that cause measles, mumps, influenza, tuberculosis, and smallpox, travel through the air, often in droplets of moisture. They can be expelled from the nose and mouth of an infected person and inhaled by anyone who is close to that person.

Other infectious diseases are spread through unclean food and polluted water. They include cholera, dysentery, and typhoid fever. Still others, such as malaria, rabies, bubonic plague, and Rocky Mountain spotted fever, are transmitted by the bites of infected animals and insects. Syphilis and gonorrhea are spread by sexual contact, as are many cases of AIDS.

To defend itself against these bacterial and viral enemies, the human body produces substances known as antibodies. There are thousands of different antibodies, each of them capable of weakening or destroying a particular disease-carrying bacterium or virus.

The mobilization of antibodies is called the body's immune response. When the response is effective, the body repels the disease and the person recovers. Since the antibodies remain in the system for a considerable period of time afterward, it is unlikely the person will get the same disease again. He or she is said to be immune to it.

Sometimes, however, the body's immune response is not strong enough to fend off the disease by itself. It needs help, and over the years medical science has developed a tremendous number of drugs and vaccines to bolster the immune system. But there remains much about the way the human body works—and the way different diseases operate—that medical science still does not know.

When a disease is common in a particular region— as measles, chickenpox, and mumps are in the Western

Hemisphere—it is said to be *endemic* to that region. New generations of children may fall victim to an endemic disease, but most adults, having survived it as children, are immune to it. Consequently, an endemic disease can usually be controlled with the aid of drugs and vaccines.

An *epidemic* disease, on the other hand, is one that spreads rapidly among many people in a community at the same time. The worst epidemics occur when a disease, such as a new type of influenza, strikes a community that has never experienced the disease before and thus has no immunity to it. Then adults as well as children are affected, and the risk of acute illness or even death is much greater.

Most epidemics are limited to a fairly small area—a city or a region. If an epidemic sweeps across an entire country, or travels from one country to another until much of the world is affected, it becomes known as a *pandemic*. The outbreak of bubonic plague in the fourteenth century, the so-called Black Death, was a pandemic. So is AIDS today.

When there is no known treatment, let alone cure, for an epidemic disease, it is often called a *plague*. One of the earliest recorded examples is the Plague of Athens. The word comes from the Latin *plaga*, which means a blow—frequently one administered by a god. Perhaps this indicates that from the start many people believed plagues were a form of divine punishment. Some still do.

Much could be written about each of the different epidemic diseases, from tuberculosis to typhus to infantile paralysis, that have caused humankind so much suffering and loss of life. This book tells the stories of three of the most serious and damaging plagues: the Black Death, which ravaged western Europe in the mid-1300s; smallpox, the only epidemic disease that has been wiped out completely; and AIDS, the modern plague whose mysteries remain to be solved. All three have had disastrous impacts on the affected populations and left lasting social, political, religious, and cultural consequences in their wake.

As each of the diseases has run its deadly course, people have reacted in similar ways. Some reached out to aid the sufferers, others fled in terror, still others searched frantically for someone or something to blame. All these reactions came into play in A.D. 1347, when the Black Death broke out for the first time in what is today southern Ukraine.

The Black Death

CHAPTER ONE

OUT OF THE EAST

Early in 1347, a mysterious disease attacked people living near the Black Sea in what is now southern Ukraine. Its victims suffered from headaches, felt weak and tired, and staggered when they tried to walk.

By the third day, the lymph nodes in the sufferers' groins, or occasionally their armpits, began to swell. Soon they reached the size of hens' eggs. These swellings became known as buboes, from the Greek word for groin, *boubon*. They gave the disease its official name: the bubonic plague.

The victim's heart beat wildly as it tried to pump blood through the swollen tissues. The nervous system started to collapse, causing dreadful pain and bizarre movements of the arms and legs. Then, as death neared, the mouth gaped open and the skin blackened from internal bleeding. The end usually came on the fifth day.

Within weeks of the first reported cases, hundreds of people in the Black Sea region had sickened and died. Those who survived were terrified. Like the citizens of Athens at the time of the Plague, they had no medicines with which to fight the disease. As it continued to spread, their fear changed to frustration, and then to anger. Someone—some outsider—must be responsible for bringing this calamity upon them.

The most likely candidates were the Italian traders who operated in the region. They bartered Italian goods for the silks and spices that came over the caravan routes from the Far East, then shipped the Eastern merchandise on to Italy. Although many of the traders had lived in the region for years, they were still thought of as being different. For one thing, they were Christians while most of the natives were Muslims.

Deciding the Italians were to blame for the epidemic, the natives gathered an army and prepared to attack their trading post. The Italians fled to a fortress they had built on the coast of the Black Sea. There the natives besieged them until the dread disease broke out in the Muslim army.

The natives were forced to withdraw. But before they did—according to one account—they gave the Italians a taste of the agony their people had been suffering. They loaded catapults with the bodies of some of their dead soldiers and hurled them over the high walls into the fortress. By doing so, they hoped to infect the Italians with the plague.

As fast as the bodies landed, the Italians dumped them into the sea. However, they did not move quickly enough, for the disease had already taken hold among them. In a panic, the traders loaded three ships and set sail for their home port of Genoa in Italy. They made it only as far as Messina, on the island of Sicily, before the rapid spread of the disease forced them to stop.

This account of what happened in southern Ukraine may or may not be true. But it is a fact that the bubonic plague—the Black Death—arrived in Sicily in October 1347, carried by the crew of a fleet from the east. All the sailors on the ships were dead or dying. In the words of a contemporary historian, they had "sickness clinging to their very bones."

The harbormasters at the port of Messina ordered the sick sailors to remain on board, hoping in this way to prevent the disease from spreading to the town. They had no way of knowing that the actual carriers of the disease had already left the ships. Under cover of night, when no one could see them, they had scurried down the ropes that tied the ships to the dock and vanished into Messina.

The carriers were black rats and the fleas that lived in their hair. Driven by an unending search for food, the rats' ancestors had migrated slowly westward along the caravan routes. They had traveled in bolts of cloth and bales of hay, and the fleas had come with them.

Although it was only an eighth of an inch long, the rat flea was a tough, adaptable creature. It depended for nourishment on the blood of its host, which it obtained through a daggerlike snout that could pierce the rat's skin. And in its stomach the flea often carried thousands of the deadly bacteria that caused the bubonic plague.

The bacteria did no apparent harm to the flea, and a black rat could tolerate a moderate amount of them, too, without showing ill effects. But sometimes the flea contained so many bacteria that they invaded the rat's lungs or nervous system when the flea injected its snout. Then the rat died a swift and horrible death, and the flea had to find a new host.

Aiding the tiny flea in its search were its powerful legs, which could jump more than 150 times the creature's length. In most instances the flea landed on another black rat. Not always, though. If most of the rats in the vacinity were already dead or dying from the plague, the flea might leap to a human being instead. As soon as it had settled on the human's skin, the flea would begin to feed, and the whole process of infection would be repeated.

No doubt it was fleas, not Italian traders, that brought the bubonic plague to the Black Sea region, and other fleas that carried the disease on to Sicily. But no one at the time made the connection. To the people of the fourteenth century, the cause of the Black Death—which they called "the pestilence"—was a complete and utter mystery.

When the first cases of the plague were reported in Messina, the authorities ordered the Italian fleet and all its sick crew members to leave the port at once. Their action came too late, however. Within days the disease had spread throughout the city and the surrounding countryside.

Some of the plague's victims fled to the nearby town of Catania, where they were treated kindly at first. But when the citizens of Catania realized how deadly the disease was, they refused to have anything more to do with anyone from Messina or even to speak to them. As was to happen wherever the plague struck, fear for one's own life usually outweighed any concern a person might have felt for the life of another.

ON TO ITALY

From Sicily, trading ships loaded with infected flea-bearing rats carried the Black Death to ports on the mainland of Italy. Peddlers and other travelers helped spread it to inland cities such as Milan and Florence.

Conditions in these medieval cities provided a splendid breeding ground for all types of vermin, including rats. There were no regular garbage collections, and refuse accumulated in piles in the streets. Rushes from wet or marshy places, not rugs, covered the floors in most homes. After a meal, it was customary to throw bits of leftover food onto the rushes for the dog or cat to eat. Rats and mice often got their share, too.

Because the cities had no running water, even the wealthy seldom washed their heavy clothing, or their own bodies. As a result, both rich and poor were prime targets for lice and fleas and the diseases they carried—the most deadly being the bubonic plague.

Several Italian commentators noted an unusual number of dead rats in cities struck by the plague. It seems odd that no one linked this phenomenon to the disease. Perhaps people were so used to being surrounded by vermin, dead and alive, that a few more didn't arouse that much concern. At any rate, the Italians sought other explanations for the terrible pestilence.

Some scholars thought the plague had been triggered by a series of earthquakes that had devastated large areas of Europe and Asia between 1345 and 1347. They said the quakes had released poisonous fumes from the Earth's core, and some believed the Devil was behind it all.

Others claimed that climatic changes had brought warmer, damper weather and strong southerly winds that carried the disease north. They tried to predict its course by studying the colors of the sky at twilight and the shapes of cloud formations. Meanwhile, the death toll in both city and countryside continued to mount.

At Venice, one of Italy's major ports, the city's leaders decreed that no one could leave an incoming ship for *quaranta giorni*—forty days—the length of time Christ was said to have suffered in the wilderness. From this decree comes the word *quarantine*, which means any isolation or restriction on travel intended to keep a contagious disease from spreading. But the quarantine in Venice proved no more effective than the one imposed earlier at Messina. When the Black Death struck in December 1347, Venice had a population of about 130,000. Eighteen months later, only about 70,000 Venetians were still alive.

Other Italian cities tried harsher measures to halt the spread of the disease. As soon as the first cases were reported in Milan, the authorities sent the city militia to wall up the houses where the victims lived. All those inside, whether sick or well, were cut off from their friends and neighbors and left to die.

The most complete account of the Black Death in

Italy was given by the writer Giovanni Boccaccio, who lived in the city of Florence. In the preface to his classic book *The Decameron*, Boccaccio wrote: "Some say that the plague descended upon the human race through the influence of the heavenly bodies, others that it was a punishment signifying God's righteous anger at our wicked way of life."

After describing the disease's symptoms, Boccaccio went on to say: "Against these maladies, it seemed that all the advice of physicians and all the power of medicine were profitless and futile. Perhaps the nature of the illness was such that it allowed no remedy; or perhaps those people who were treating the illness, being ignorant of its causes, were not prescribing the appropriate cure."

One of the most alarming things about the bubonic plague was the way it struck. "It would rush upon its victims with the speed of a fire racing through dry or oily substances that happened to be placed within its reach," Boccaccio wrote. "Not only did it infect healthy persons who conversed or had any dealings with the sick . . . but it also seemed to transfer the sickness to anyone touching the clothes or the other objects which had been handled or used by the victims."

Boccaccio reported seeing two pigs in the street, rooting through the ragged clothes of a poor man who had died of the plague. Within a short time, the pigs began to writhe and squirm as though they had been poisoned. Then they both dropped dead, falling on the same rags they had been pulling and tugging a few minutes earlier.

How did the people of Florence react to this mysterious and fatal disease? Some isolated themselves in their homes, according to Boccaccio. They ate lightly, saw no outsiders, and refused to receive reports of the dead or sick. Others adopted an attitude of "play today for we die tomorrow." They drank heavily, stayed out late, and roamed through the streets singing and dancing as if the Black Death were an enormous joke. Still others, if they were rich enough, abandoned their homes in the city and fled to villas in the countryside. They hoped in this way to escape the disease—but often it followed them.

Whatever steps they took, the same percentage of people in each group seemed to fall ill. So many died that the bodies piled up in the streets. A new occupation came into being: that of loading the bodies on carts and carrying them away for burial in mass graves. "No more respect was accorded to dead people," Boccaccio wrote, "than would be shown toward dead goats."

The town of Siena, thirty miles south of Florence, suffered severe losses also. A man named Agnolo di Tura offered a vivid account of what happened there:

"The mortality in Siena began in May. It was a horrible thing, and I do not know where to begin to tell of the cruelty. . . . Members of a household brought their dead to a ditch as best they could, without a priest, without any divine services. Nor did the death bell sound. . . . And as soon as those ditches were filled, more were dug. I, Agnolo di Tura, buried my five children with my own hands. . . . And no bells tolled, and nobody wept no matter what his loss because almost everyone expected death. . . . And people said and believed, 'This is the end of the world.' "

By the winter of 1348–49, a little more than a year after its first appearance in Sicily, the worst of the Black Death was over in Italy. No one knows exactly how many Italians died of the disease, because accurate medical records were not kept. Conservative estimates put the loss at about a third of the population, but many scholars believe the death rate reached forty or fifty percent, especially in the cities.

In any case, it was the greatest loss of human life Italy had suffered in a comparable period of time—and a loss not equaled to the present day.

Meanwhile, the Black Death had swept on to France, entering that country via Marseilles and other southern ports. Before long it traveled inland and reached the city of Avignon, where the Pope was then living.

CHAPTER TWO

BETWEEN TWO RAGING FIRES

When the Black Death arrived in Avignon in the spring of 1348, this old walled city in southern France had been the home of the Pope and his College of Cardinals for almost forty years. They had come there in 1309 to escape political unrest in Rome and had built a magnificent palace on the city's main square.

Pilgrims, priests, and diplomats crowded into Avignon from all over Europe to pay their respects to the Pope. Without meaning to, some of these visitors must have brought the pestilence with them. Between February and May, up to 400 people a day died of the plague in Avignon. When the graveyards were filled, the bodies of the dead had to be dumped into the Rhône River, which flowed through the heart of the city.

Many courageous priests ministered to the sick and dying even though they knew that they would probably become infected and die themselves. Meanwhile, Pope Clement VI decided it was his duty, as leader of the Roman Catholic Church on the Earth, to remain alive if at all possible. On the advice of his physician, he withdrew to his private rooms, saw nobody, and spent day and night between two fires that blazed on grates at opposite ends of his bedchamber.

What purpose were the fires supposed to serve? It was tied in with the theory of humors, which still dominated medical thought in the fourteenth century. This theory goes back to the Greek physician Hippocrates, who lived from about 484 to 425 B.C. and is often called the "father of medicine."

Hippocrates examined sick persons carefully and honestly recorded the signs and symptoms of various diseases. But his knowledge of how the human body worked was extremely limited. He believed the body contained four basic liquids, which he called humors: blood, which came from the heart; phlegm, from the brain; yellow bile, from the liver; and black bile, from the spleen.

If these humors were in balance, Hippocrates wrote, a person would enjoy good health. But if one of them became more important than the others, the person was likely to feel pain and fall victim to a disease.

A physician's main job, therefore, was to try to restore and maintain a proper balance among the four humors.

BLOOD AND BILE

Another Greek physician, Galen (A.D.130–200), took the ideas of Hippocrates a step further. Galen stated that the four humors in the human body reflected the four elements that people believed were the basis of all life: earth, air, fire, and water. Blood was hot and moist, like the air in summer. Phlegm was cold and moist, like water. Yellow bile was hot and dry, like fire, and black bile was cold and dry, like earth. In other words, according to Galen, the human body was a smaller, contained version of the wider natural world.

Galen recommended certain treatments to keep the humors in balance. For example, if a patient was too hot, various foods were prescribed to make him or her cooler. If this treatment failed, the physician might perform bloodletting to reduce the amount of hot blood in the patient's system.

Most of Galen's theories have been discredited in modern times, but for over a thousand years, until the sixteenth century, no physician thought of questioning them. There were several reasons why this was so. One was the fact that the Roman Catholic Church led the way in education as well as religion during the Middle Ages.

Convinced that everything in the world was under divine control, Church leaders frowned on independent thought and scientific experimentation. In 1300, for example, Pope Boniface III decreed that anyone who dared to cut up a dead human body would be banned from the Church. This edict in effect outlawed the dissection of corpses in medical schools and prevented students from gaining a better understanding of the body's organs and how they were related. Any dissection that was done had to be performed on the bodies of pigs, not people.

In this climate, it was easier for physicians to rely on Galen, who seemed to have an explanation for everything, than pursue original medical investigations of their own. Most medieval physicians were actually scholar-priests. They spent their time analyzing the writings of Galen and Hippocrates and left the treatment of patients to surgeons and barber-surgeons.

Surgeons usually had some medical training in a university. They were regarded as skilled craftsmen, able to close wounds, set broken bones, and perform simple operations.

Most barber-surgeons were illiterate men whose only training came from serving as apprentices to surgeons. As their name implies, they cut hair as well as setting simple fractures and bandaging wounds. Some say the traditional red-and-white-striped barber's pole comes from the time when barber-surgeons hung their bloody surgical rags in front of their shops to dry.

Two other groups of people played important roles in medieval medicine. Apothecaries filled prescriptions and also prescribed herbs and drugs on their own. Nonprofessionals, many of them older women, provided medical care in rural areas where no surgeons or barber-surgeons were available. These nonprofessionals had no formal training and relied heavily on folk remedies that had been handed down from generation to generation in the countryside.

STRANGE TREATMENTS

This, then, was the medical scene when the Black Death raged through western Europe in the mid-fourteenth century. It helps to explain why physicians and surgeons were at such a loss to know what caused the epidemic, let alone how to treat it. It also answers the question of why the Pope's physician had him sit alone in his bedchamber between two raging fires.

Galen had written that diseases were transmitted from person to person by miasmas, poisonous vapors that arose from swamps and corrupted the air. The Pope's physician, who believed in Galen's theories, thought that hot air from the fires would combat any dangerous miasmas that got into the Pope's chamber and render them harmless. (The Pope did survive, but it's doubtful whether the fires had anything to do with it except to make his chamber uncomfortable for rats and fleas.)

Other physicians and surgeons interpreted Galen's theories differently. Instead of fighting fire with fire, so to speak, they recommended fleeing from it. People were urged to leave warm, low, marshy places that were likely to produce miasmas and move to drier, cooler regions in the hills. If that was not possible, they were advised to stay indoors during the heat of the day, cover over any brightly lighted windows, and try to stay cool.

Hands and feet were to be washed regularly, but physicians warned against bathing the body because it opened the pores. This, they thought, made the body more vulnerable to attack by disease-bearing miasmas. Exercise was to be avoided for the same reason.

Sleep after eating and in the middle of the day was bad because the body was warmer then. And physicians cautioned their patients not to sleep on their backs at any time, because that made it easier for foul air to flow down their nostrils and get into their lungs.

To ward off miasmas when one walked outside, physicians recommended carrying bouquets of sweet-smelling herbs and flowers and holding them up to the nose. Some say this practice was one of the inspirations for the old English nursery rhyme "Ring-a-ring o' roses." In the first published version it read as follows:

Ring-a-ring o' roses,
A pocket full of posies,
A-tishoo! A-tishoo!
We all fall down.

Those who link the rhyme to the plague think the ring o' roses was the rash that often signaled infection. The pocket full of posies referred to the flowers people carried to sweeten the air around them. A-tishoo! was the sound of sneezing, a common symptom of the disease, and "We all fall down" implied that all of its victims died.

Some prescribed treatments for the plague seem sensible or at least harmless: bed rest, drinking lots of liquids, and the application of salves made of herbs to the affected areas of the body. But other treatments hurt plague sufferers instead of helping them.

Surgeons who had studied Galen's theories believed that the Black Death interrupted the flow of the body's humors. Since the heart produced the most important of these liquids, blood, doctors thought one effective way to fight the plague and improve circulation was to bleed veins close to the heart.

The surgeons also thought that buboes, the swellings that characterized the disease, revealed where the body was being attacked, and they geared their treatment accordingly. If a buboe appeared in the region of the groin, for example, the surgeon drained blood from a vein leading to one of the organs in that area. By doing so, the surgeon meant to cool the body and help it fight the disease, but in fact bleeding only weakened the body's defenses.

ST. ROCH

In the face of treatments like these, it's no wonder that people lost faith in their physicians and came to rely more and more on prayer. Many directed their prayers to St. Roch, who had died in 1327 and was the particular saint associated with the plague.

According to the legends told about him in France and Italy, Roch inherited great wealth as a young man. Like St. Francis, he gave it away to the poor and then went on a religious pilgrimage to Italy. He was in Rome when an epidemic struck, but instead of fleeing, Roch stayed on to nurse the sick. Eventually, he caught the disease himself.

Roch left the city and went to the countryside, where he expected to die alone in the woods. But a dog carrying a loaf of bread in its mouth miraculously found him. Each day the dog reappeared with a fresh loaf, and Roch gradually recovered.

He got home to France safely, but his relatives failed to recognize him and had Roch arrested as an impostor. He died in jail, filling his cell with a mysterious white light. After Roch's story spread and he was made a saint, it was thought he would come to the aid of plague victims just as the dog had come to his aid in the Roman woods.

Even prayers to St. Roch did not halt the relentless march of the Black Death through France, however. At the peak of the plague, the death rate in Paris was reported to be 800 a day. By the time the epidemic had run its course in 1349, over 50,000 Parisians had died—half the city's population.

Meanwhile, the Black Death had crossed the English Channel and was wreaking fresh havoc in the British Isles.

CHAPTER THREE

LOOKING FOR SCAPEGOATS

From a distance, the English village looked calm and peaceful under the summer sun of 1349. The thatched roofs of its cottages seemed to glisten in the haze. Beyond the cottages, the grass in the village pastureland was a lush green, and the oak trees in the wood were thick with leaves.

But a visitor who came closer would have seen that all was not well in the village. The doors of some cottages hung open, revealing that the inhabitants had fled in haste. From other dwellings came the moans of people in pain. A woman who had just drawn water from the village well collapsed from fever or fatigue when she tried to lift her bucket.

The sense of dread and decay was even more noticeable in the fields around the village. Weeds crowded out the growing crops of oats and barley, indicating that no one had cultivated them in some time. Two pigs were loose in the vegetable garden, rooting among the beans and cabbages. A cow had wandered off into the woods.

This was a typical scene in the English countryside the year the Black Death struck. Nearly ninety percent of the population lived in villages ranging in size from large ones containing 500 or more inhabitants to small ones made up of just ten or twelve families. Large or small, they were all affected by the plague.

Henry Knighton, a clergyman at Leicester Abbey, left an eyewitness account of the damage. He wrote: "Sheep and cattle were left to wander through the fields and among the standing crops since there was no one to drive them off or collect them. For want of people to look after them they died in hedgerows and ditches all over the country.

"So few servants and laborers were left that nobody knew where to turn for help. The following autumn it was not possible to get a harvester except by paying eight pence a day [a large amount then] with food included. Because of this, many crops were left to rot in the fields."

Another chronicler, from an abbey near the town of Lincoln, wrote an even more vivid account of the plague's ravages. "It filled the whole world with terror," he said. "In places not even a fifth part of the people were left alive. So great an epidemic has never been seen nor heard of before this time, for it is believed that even the waters of the flood which happened in the days of Noah did not carry off so vast a multitude."

In the face of such horror, some people blamed themselves for the epidemic. "This surely must be caused by the sins of men," said the Archbishop of York. He urged his followers to join in group prayers and religious processions in an attempt to ward off the pestilence.

Others, like the residents along the Black Sea who were among the first victims of the Black Death, looked for someone else to blame. An outsider, or just someone who was "different."

On the edges of many villages, in poor huts made of sticks and straw, lived outcasts of various kinds. Some were deformed from birth, others were simple-minded, still others were insane. The villagers gave them names like Poor Tom or Mad Mag. The majority were harmless, although children sometimes taunted them and called the old women witches. Most adults simply left them alone.

That changed when the Black Death came. As more people sickened and died, the survivors became increasingly frustrated. Neither the village priest nor the barber-surgeon had a solution for the plague. In many instances, they were among its victims. Maybe the children were right, the fearful survivors thought. Maybe Mad Mag really was a witch. If they got rid of her, maybe the pestilence would finally go away. . . .

At the height of the plague, there were reports from many English villages of local eccentrics being stoned or beaten to death by crowds of their angry, frightened neighbors. But the worst cases of such violence occurred in Germany when the Black Death arrived there.

THE FLAGELLANTS

One group of Germans carried self-blame to its furthest extreme. These were the people known as the Flagellants because they literally whipped themselves. Small bands of Flagellants had roamed across central Europe for years, seeking God's forgiveness by punishing themselves for their sins. The number of participants increased dramatically during the years of the Black Death.

The Flagellants were organized in groups of several hundred or more under the leadership of a man they called "Master" or "Father." Each member of the group swore obedience to the master for a period of 33½ days—representing the number of years Jesus Christ was said to have lived on the Earth. During that time the Flagellants could not bathe, shave, or sleep on soft beds, and they could not speak to anyone without the permission of the Master.

Dressed in hooded white robes with red fabric crosses sewn on the front and back, the Flagellants went from town to town in long, winding processions. They walked two by two, the men in front, the women bringing up the rear. When they came to a new town, they made their way to the biggest church, which was usually located on the central square. There each man removed his outer robe and, wearing only a long, skirt-like garment, prepared to begin the standard ritual.

They marched slowly in a circle around the Master, crying aloud to God to spare them and singing hymns. All the while they beat their bare backs and shoulders with leather whips tipped with small iron spikes. Often the spikes drew blood, which only made the Flagellants sing and chant more loudly. In their suffering, they believed they were reenacting Christ's agony on the cross. At last, on a signal from the Master, they all fell to the ground and lay face downward, sobbing.

Twice each day the Flagellants performed this rite while a crowd of townspeople looked on. Some were frightened by the Flagellants, but the majority of Germans admired them. They invited the Flagellants into their homes, provided them with food, and gave them candles for their rites—all in the hope that the Flagellants' self-punishing behavior would persuade God to halt the plague.

In time, though, the Flagellants went too far. The warm reception they received in town after town made them think they could do anything they wanted. They even challenged the Roman Catholic Church, interrupting religious services, stealing valuables, and claiming that they, not the priests of the Church, were the true representatives of God on the Earth.

At last Pope Clement acted. In October 1349 he issued a bull, or decree, condemning flagellantism and urging authorities everywhere to outlaw the Flagellants and their cruel rituals.

The Pope's decree was heeded quickly, and by 1350 the Flagellant movement had been almost completely wiped out in western Europe. In the meantime, though, the Flagellants had stirred up trouble of a different kind. Having failed through their actions to slow or stop the plague, the Flagellants needed a scapegoat—someone or something to bear the blame for their failure. They found a convenient target: the Jews.

THE FIRST HOLOCAUST

For centuries the Jews of Europe had been treated like outcasts. Christianity was the official religion in most western European countries, and the Jews were scorned as nonbelievers. They were called Christ killers or worse. Some Church officials even claimed that Jews kidnapped and tortured Christian children in reenactments of the Crucifixion.

Because they were considered to be aliens, Jews enjoyed no civil rights. They were banned from all government posts, could not serve in the army or own land, and were not permitted to work as craftsmen. In 1213, Pope Innocent III decreed that both sexes, from the age of seven or eight, had to wear circular badges of yellow felt that identified them as Jews. (Almost six hundred years after the arrival of the Black Plague, in the 1930s and 1940s, the Nazis made the Jews of Germany and the occupied countries wear similar yellow emblems in the shape of a six-pointed Star of David.)

One of the few occupations open to Jews was moneylending. This was because the Church forbade Christians from using money to make money. However, the Jews had to charge interest rates of twenty percent or more in order to pay the high taxes levied on their businesses. These rates angered the people who came to the Jews for loans, and made them more willing to believe the rumors—spread by the Flagellants and others—that the Jews were responsible for the Black Death.

According to the rumors, the Jews were polluting the wells in Christian communities with poisons imported from Moorish Spain and the Far East. If Christians drank water from the wells, the rumormongers claimed, they would be infected with the plague and die.

It's hard to know why these rumors started, since no one who had spoken or written of the pestilence asserted that it was caused by impure water. Perhaps they came from the fact that the Jews' religious laws made them more aware of hygiene. Consequently, they often avoided using wells that were close to sewage pits and obtained water instead from clear streams and springs, even if it meant going farther from their homes.

Whatever the explanation, the rumors led to eleven Jews being put on trial in September 1348. They were charged with having poisoned the wells in a small south German town. After hours of painful torture, the eleven confessed to the deed and said they had received the poison from a rabbi in Spain.

The confessions were false, of course, wrung out of the Jews by their torturers. But that made no difference to those who wanted to believe the worst of them. All eleven men were condemned to death, and news of their trial set off a wave of repression and terror in other German and Swiss cities.

In January 1349, the two hundred Jewish residents of Basel, Switzerland, were herded into a wooden building on an island in the Rhine River and burned alive. Protesting their innocence to the end, Jews were put to death in one city after another. At the town of Speyer, bodies of murdered Jews were packed into huge, empty wine casks and sent floating off down the Rhine.

In most places, the massacres occurred while the Black Death was attacking the population, but in some cities word that the disease was coming was enough to arouse the citizens. On February 14, 1349, several weeks before the first cases of bubonic plague were reported there, two thousand Jews were killed in the city of Strassburg. As the Jews marched under guard through the city on their way to the execution ground, some members of the watching crowd tore the clothes off the Jews' backs. They thought they might find gold pieces hidden in the linings.

Some Christians tried to stop the slaughter. Pope Clement VI, from his residence in Avignon, condemned the killings and sent messages urging his followers to behave with tolerance toward the Jews. He and others pointed out that, proportionately, as many Jews had fallen victim to the plague as Christians. But the Pope's words were drowned out by continuing cries for revenge against the so-called poisoners of the wells.

In August 1349, mobs led by the Flagellants moved against the Jews in the large German cities of Cologne and Mainz. At Mainz, the Jews rebelled and attacked their oppressors, killing two hundred according to one chronicler. Overpowered at last by the larger force of Christians, the Jews retreated to their homes and set them on fire. Three thousand Jews were said to have died in the blazing houses rather than be killed by their enemies.

AFTER THE HORROR

The persecution of the Jews, in Germany and elsewhere, ended only when the death rate from the plague began to decline. By then, it is believed, over 200 Jewish communities had been completely wiped out and 350 other massacres of Jews had taken place. Not until the Nazi Holocaust during World War II would the Jewish people again suffer such overwhelming losses.

Many of the survivors fled Germany and moved to eastern Europe. A large number settled in Poland, where King Casimir offered them special protection. As the Jews labored to rebuild their lives, they tried to forget the horrors of the Black Death. So did the rest of Europe, but it was impossible to ignore the hard facts of the epidemic.

Before the plague, historians estimate, Europe had a population of about 75 million. In 1351, after the disease seemed to have run its course, Pope Clement's agents calculated that 23,840,000 people had died of it—almost thirty-two percent of the population. This figure echoes the words of the contemporary chronicler Jean Froissart, who wrote: "A third of the world died."

As things turned out, Froissart spoke too soon. For although the worst was over by 1351, the Black Death didn't stay away. It broke out again in various parts of Europe at least once every ten years until the end of the century. Especially hard hit were the young who had not been exposed to the disease before.

None of the later epidemics was as widespread as the first, and when the disease ran out of fresh victims it finally eased its grip in the early 1400s. By that time Europe's population had been reduced by nearly fifty percent.

The incredibly high death toll was just one of the plague's consequences. Like a revolution or a world war, the Black Death had a profound and lasting effect on every area of human activity.

CHAPTER FOUR

A CHANGED WORLD

Once they got over their grief at the loss of loved ones and began to pick up the threads of their daily lives, the survivors of the Black Death realized that many things in the world had changed. Not just in the immediate environment, but in their deepest thoughts and feelings.

The most obvious changes affected their livelihoods. If they were nobles, used to having hundreds of poorly paid serfs to farm their lands, they were faced with a severe labor shortage due to deaths from the plague. Those who rounded up help and put in crops then discovered there wasn't as big a market for them—again because of the plague. Agricultural prices fell as a result, further weakening the nobles whose power and wealth depended on the value of their landholdings.

The serfs, on the other hand, found themselves in a much stronger position after the plague. With their services in demand, many in England and elsewhere ran away from the estates to which they had been bound since birth. They either sought out other estates, where they could bargain for better wages and live as free men, or went to cities like London in hope of learning a trade.

As wages rose, even the poor enjoyed a higher standard of living. They ate better foods than before and wore finer clothing. For the first time in England, members of the working classes were seen in fur coats of sheep or lambskin. Until then only nobles and high-ranking clergymen could afford to wear furs.

A LOSS OF FAITH

Another major change occurred in the way people viewed the Roman Catholic Church. Before the Black Death, most Europeans accepted without question the word of the Church, as expressed by its bishops and priests. The plague shattered that faith. While some priests sacrificed their lives to aid the sick and dying, others fled or isolated themselves. Whether they stayed or fled, it soon became apparent that none of them could explain why God had permitted such devastation.

After the worst was over, the survivors felt a strong

need for religious belief and hoped their faith in God and the Church might be restored. But, like the serfs, many of the remaining priests left their posts in the countryside and went to towns and cities in search of wealthier parishes. The English poet William Langland wrote about this unfortunate trend in his classic work, *Piers Plowman*.

> Parsons and parish priests complained to the Bishop
> That their parishes were poor since the pestilence time
> And asked leave and licence in London to dwell
> And sing requiems for stipends, since silver is sweet.

Pope Clement responded angrily to such behavior. "What can you preach to the people?" he asked his bishops in 1351. "If on humility, you yourselves are the proudest of the world, arrogant and given to pomp. If on poverty, you are the most grasping and the most covetous. . . ."

Despite these rumblings of discontent, the Church continued to be one of the most powerful forces in fourteenth-century Europe. However, it never regained the complete authority it had enjoyed before the plague. Once people began to question the Church's actions, they kept on questioning them. This eventually led to attempts to reform the Roman Catholic Church and then, in the sixteenth century, to the establishment of the first Protestant churches.

MORE QUESTIONS

In the meantime, a questioning mood spread to other fields after the plague. Among them was medicine. Because Galen's theories and recommended treatments had failed to prevent or cure the disease, doctors gradually turned away from them in the years following the epidemic. Instead of analyzing Galen's philosophy, medical students at the University of Paris and other institutions took practical courses in anatomy and surgery. Despite continuing objections from the Church, the students were permitted to dissect human bodies as part of their studies.

For the first time, medical textbooks were published in English, French, German, and Italian rather than Latin, which only university-educated physicians could understand. Now ordinary men and women had access to medical guides and could begin to take control of their own health.

To help restore the average person's confidence in the medical profession, doctors were asked to obey a code of ethics. One French code, proposed by Guy de Chauliac, sounds remarkably up-to-date. Here are some of its rules:

"The doctor should be well mannered . . . and abhor false cures or practices. He should be affable to the sick, kindhearted to his colleagues, wise in his prognostications. He should not be grasping in money matters, and then he will receive a salary commensurate with his labors, the financial ability of his patients, and the success of the treatment. . . ."

In medicine, as in other fields of study, there was a new emphasis on what is called the "scientific method." Rather than rely on answers from some higher authority, followers of this method put forward a theory as to why something in nature works the way it does. Then they test the theory by careful observation and analysis until they are able to prove or disprove it.

The scientific method encouraged European scholars to abandon their outworn ideas in favor of risk taking and experimentation. This new daring led in turn to the great discoveries in technology, geography, and navigation that marked the following century.

This is not to say that Gutenberg wouldn't have invented movable type in 1456 or Columbus have sailed across the Atlantic to the Caribbean islands in 1492 if the Black Death hadn't cleared the way for a new spirit in science. But it can't be disputed that, by turning the old world upside down, the Black Death helped pave the way for the new.

CHAPTER FIVE

THE PLAGUE RETURNS

Although the bubonic plague never again claimed as many victims as in the fourteenth century, it had by no means vanished from the Earth. The disease recurred here and there throughout mainland Europe and Great Britain during the 1500s. In 1664 it struck the city of London with such ferocity that the outbreak became known as the Great Plague. Out of a population estimated at 460,000, almost 70,000 Londoners died.

King Charles, his family, and his staff left London for Hampton Court Palace. Many other city dwellers followed the king to the countryside. Shopkeepers went bankrupt for lack of customers.

Servants dismissed by their employers who had left London were hired by the city to drive "dead carts"

that carried the bodies of the plague's victims to ceme-
teries. All day long the carts rumbled through the city
streets while their drivers shouted, "Bring out your
dead!"

The Lord Mayor of London ordered all dogs and
cats in the city to be killed because it was thought they
were spreading the disease. Within days, officials announced that 40,000 dogs and perhaps five times as
many cats had been destroyed. But instead of halting
the plague, this slaughter only enabled it to spread more
rapidly. For with the cats gone, the city's rats—the true
carriers of the plague—could thrive and multiply.

The London Board of Health believed, mistakenly,
that most cases of the disease were transmitted person
to person, from infected individuals to healthy ones.
So when someone was diagnosed as having the plague,
the Board enforced a strict forty-day quarantine on the
person's house. A large red cross was painted on the
front door, warning others to stay away, and guards
were posted outside to make sure no one entered or
left.

The living conditions inside a marked house soon
became unbearable, and sometimes friends or neighbors helped the inhabitants to escape. The English
writer Samuel Pepys recorded one such instance in his
famous diary:

September 3, 1665 (Lord's Day: Sunday)

I [went] up to the Vestry at the desire of the Justices of the Peace, in order to the doing [of] something for the keeping of the plague from growing. . . . Among other stories, one was very passionate, methought, of a complaint brought against a man in the town for taking a child from London from an infected house.

Alderman Hooker told us it was the child of a very able citizen in Gracious Street, a saddler, who had buried all the rest of his children of the plague, and himself and wife now being shut up and in despair of escaping, did desire only to save the life of this little child; and so prevailed to have it received stark-naked into the arms of a friend, who brought it (having put it into new fresh clothes) to Greenwich; where upon hearing the story, we did agree it should be permitted to be received and kept in the town.

Pepys, an important official in the British Naval Department, remained in London for most of the plague's duration and often commented on its ravages. Although Pepys didn't say so, the parents in the above story probably removed their child's clothing before handing it over for fear the garments were contaminated.

In the late fall of 1665, the death rate from the plague in London declined abruptly: During the last week in September, 4,929 people had died; by the end of November, the toll dropped to 900 a week. People began to return to the city. On Christmas morning, Pepys was pleased to see a jolly wedding party passing in front of his house.

UNDER CONTROL

By 1750, the bubonic plague had gradually faded out in western Europe. The last flare-ups occurred in the eastern Mediterranean ports where the disease had surfaced four hundred years earlier.

For the next hundred years, only scattered cases of plague were reported. Then, in the mid-1800s, there were fresh outbreaks in the interior of China. They failed to attract much attention in the outside world until the disease reached the port cities of Canton and Hong Kong in 1894.

Because these cities had trading contacts with Europe and the Americas as well as Asia, fears arose that a new worldwide pandemic might be starting. But medical science had made many advances since the time of the Black Death and the Great Plague of London. As a result of the pioneering work of Louis Pasteur and Robert Koch, medical researchers now had the weapons they needed to battle the bubonic plague.

Pasteur had shown that harmful bacteria could

produce disease, and Koch had discovered the specific bacteria that caused such diseases as anthrax and tuberculosis. Applying their methods, scientists from Japan and Switzerland examined plague victims in the Far East and succeeded for the first time in isolating the bacterium that caused the Black Death. Moreover, they were the first to observe that rats played a key role in transmitting the disease.

Within the next few years, other scientists working in India and what is now Taiwan grew the plague bacteria in rat fleas and demonstrated how it was transmitted from rodents to human beings. Their findings were discounted at first, however, because many authorities still believed the prime means of transmission was person to person.

This was the attitude that prevailed in San Francisco between 1900 and 1904, when 121 cases of bubonic plague were reported and all but three of the victims died. City health officials refused to accept the idea that the disease was transmitted from rat to flea to human. Instead, they quarantined or kept under close watch thousands of Asian immigrants. Like the Jews in Germany at the time of the Black Death, the unfortunate Asians were suspected of being responsible for the plague.

Only after these harsh measures failed to halt the disease did the officials heed the scientists' advice.

They ordered that all incoming and outgoing ships be disinfected, and organized massive sanitation cleanups in which approximately 700,000 rats were trapped and destroyed in San Francisco. They also lifted the restrictions on the city's Asian population.

The last sizable plague epidemic in the United States occurred in Los Angeles in 1924–25. Forty people contracted the disease, and only two of them survived it. With the development of antibiotic drugs in the 1940s, this plague became a treatable disease at last. The prompt use of streptomycin has reduced the death rate from bubonic plague to five percent.

The disease remains a threat in those parts of the world where sanitary conditions are poor and antibiotics are not readily available. India, for example, experienced an epidemic of pneumonic plague, an even deadlier form of bubonic plague, as recently as September 1994. The pneumonic form occurs when plague bacteria spread from the lymph nodes to the lungs, causing pneumonia. Unlike bubonic plague, the pneumonic form can be transmitted easily from person to person through droplets in the air.

The outbreak in India began in the industrial city of Surat, about 200 miles north of Bombay. After the first plague deaths were reported, officials in Surat closed all public gathering places, including schools, restaurants, movie theaters, and parks. As rumors circulated that hundreds had died, more than 200,000 panicky residents of Surat fled the city by bus, train, and car, just as residents of Florence, Milan, and other Italian cities fled to the countryside at the time of the Black Death.

Indian health officials took immediate steps to combat the disease. They sent millions of tablets of the antibiotic drug tetracycline to hospitals and clinics in Surat, and distributed hundreds of tons of DDT and other insecticides to kill the fleas that were spreading the disease. They also hired temporary rat catchers to trap and destroy as many members as possible of Surat's huge rat population.

Within two weeks, the situation seemed to be stabilizing. Although 54 people had died of the plague and thousands more remained in hospital isolation wards, anxiety about the epidemic had decreased. Most of the residents of Surat had returned to their homes, and no confirmed cases of the disease had been found in other Indian cities. "The Indian government has successfully controlled the epidemic," a New Delhi representative of the World Health Organization declared.

This epidemic had been curbed, but there was no assurance that another outbreak would not occur in India or some other part of the world where conditions for the disease were favorable. It's unlikely, though, that an epidemic of bubonic or pneumonic plague could ever again attain the scale of the Black Death.

While the plague was regularly attacking people throughout the world, another scourge was also bedeviling humankind. There was never a single pandemic of this disease as overwhelming as the Black Death, but it probably claimed even more victims in the long run. Especially hard hit were children.

This scourge was smallpox.

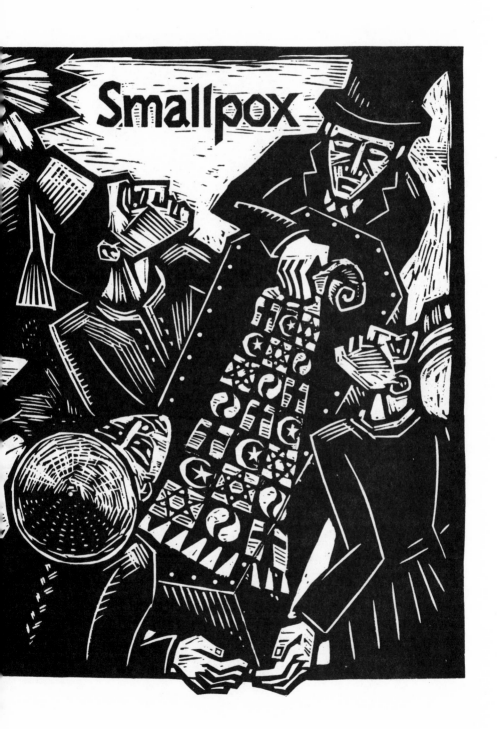

CHAPTER SIX

THE MYSTERIOUS DEATH OF A PHARAOH

In 1157 B.C., the Egyptian pharaoh Ramses V died suddenly from what his scribes called simply "an acute illness." He was only thirty and had ruled Egypt for just four years.

Mystery surrounds Ramses's death and burial. Pharaohs were usually interred after seventy days of carefully prescribed mummification procedures, but Ramses's mummy wasn't buried for almost two years. What could have caused the delay?

Twentieth-century scientists who have examined the pharaoh's well-preserved mummy believe they may have found the answer. Inspection revealed a rash of raised pustules—large pimples—on Ramses's lower face, neck, and shoulders as well as his arms. Such pustules are a typical symptom of smallpox.

Unfortunately, the pharaoh's physicians left no

written description of his illness. But if he did, in fact, die of smallpox, it would explain why it took so long for him to be embalmed and buried. Corpses of small-pox victims, and even their clothing or bedding, can transmit the disease. So the pharaoh's embalmers might have put off mummifying him until they could be certain his remains were no longer contagious.

Or perhaps the first team of embalmers contracted smallpox themselves, and fear of the disease—or a shortage of embalmers—caused a delay in the mummi-fication.

There is little hard evidence about the origins of small-pox. It probably first became a common disease among humans in ancient Egypt sometime before 1500 B.C. From there it eventually spread throughout the world, causing the deaths of millions. The English historian Thomas Babington Macaulay called it "the most terri-ble of all the ministers of death."

Smallpox was caused by a virus—but that wasn't discovered until the nineteenth century. Most of the disease's victims acquired the virus as a result of face-to-face contact with an infected person. The sufferer gave off millions of tiny virus particles when he or she sneezed or coughed, and the victim inhaled them.

During the first week after infection, there were no obvious signs of illness. Then, sometime between the ninth and twelfth days, the first symptoms appeared: high fever, chills, backache, and headache. The victim's temperature might jump to as high as 106° F.

At the end of this stage, four days or so later, the temperature dropped and the patient began to feel a little better. But any relief was only temporary, for the patient soon broke out in the smallpox rash. It usually started on the face, then spread to the chest, the arms, the back, and finally the legs.

Over the next several days, the flat spots of rash gradually turned into raised, blisterlike pustules like those found on the mummy of Ramses V. Some patients looked as if they had been badly burned. Even those who weren't as seriously affected said their skin felt as if it were on fire.

The pustules gave the disease the name by which it was first known in the West: *variola*. This came from the Latin word *varius*, meaning spotted, or from another Latin word, *varus*, meaning pimple. Variola wasn't called smallpox until the early sixteenth century, when another disease, syphilis, spread throughout Europe and the British Isles. Since syphilis in its early stages produced a similar rash, English-speaking people labeled it "the great pox" to distinguish it from variola, which they began to call "the small pox."

After about nine days, the smallpox postules split open and started to dry up. They formed scabs that eventually fell off, very often leaving the victim with deep-pitted scars on the face and body. The scars would remain there for the rest of the person's life.

That is, if he or she was lucky enough to survive the disease. In addition to the skin, the virus often attacked the eyes, throat, lungs, heart, and liver. A victim might lose the sight in one or both eyes, or might die from the virus's assault on the internal organs. The majority of deaths occurred late in the second week of the disease, after the pustules had developed, but some victims died even before the rash appeared.

SMALLPOX IN THE FAR EAST

After smallpox became established as an endemic disease in ancient Egypt, it apparently traveled eastward along the trade routes to Persia and India. One of the oldest Indian medical books, written about A.D. 400, describes the outbreak of a disease that sounds remarkably like smallpox:

> The pustules are red, yellow, and white and they are accompanied with burning pain. . . . The skin seems studded with grains of rice.

In an attempt to ward off the disease's ravages, the Indians created a smallpox goddess, whom they worshipped for centuries. The goddess's name was Sitala, which means "the cool one." The name suggested that she had the power to relieve the high fever and hot flashes that accompanied the disease.

Indian art portrayed Sitala as a woman dressed in red, the color of fire, and riding an ass. In one hand she carried a broom to sweep the disease along, and in the other a pot of cool water to soothe its feverish victims.

Indians believed that Sitala had an evil as well as a kindly side. According to the stories they told about her, she was ill-tempered and filled with a desire for revenge against humanity. She attacked children with smallpox more often than adults because in doing so she struck a blow at the future of the community.

Temples dedicated to the smallpox goddess could be found all over India. In them, worshippers prayed, "O kind Sitala, keep away from us!" An annual festival was held on the goddess's feast day. Cooking and other activities requiring heat were avoided on that day, and Indians consumed only cold food and drink for fear of annoying Sitala.

Smallpox was probably introduced into China by the Huns, a fierce race of nomads who invaded the northern part of the country about A.D. 250. As a consequence, the Chinese called the disease "Hunpox."

The new disease spread quickly, and in response the Chinese—like the Indians—invented a smallpox goddess. By worshipping her, the Chinese hoped to lessen the impact of the disease and save lives. They referred to smallpox pustules as "beautiful flowers" so as not to offend the goddess.

The Chinese believed their smallpox goddess took particular delight in scarring the faces of attractive children. This was most likely to happen, they thought, on the last night of the year. So on that night Chinese children wore ugly paper masks to bed, hoping to trick the goddess into ignoring them.

As added insurance, many children hung empty gourds near their beds on the year's last night. If the goddess entered their rooms, they prayed she would drop her smallpox rash into the gourds instead of depositing it on their skins.

When a Chinese family was struck by smallpox, they set up a drawing or painting of the goddess in their home and made offerings to it. If the patient recovered, this temporary shrine was carried from the home in a specially made paper chair or boat and reverently burned. But if the sick person died, the shrine was torn apart and the spirit of the goddess was driven away from the house with curses.

THE "RED TREATMENT"

There weren't many reports in Europe of a disease resembling smallpox during the first centuries of the Christian era. Then, in A.D. 580 and 581, a deadly illness that sounds much like smallpox swept across northern Italy and southern France. A French bishop, Gregory of Tours, left an account of this epidemic. In it, he described the corpse of a dead nobleman so covered with pustules that "it appeared black and burnt, as if it had been laid on a coal fire."

However, the bishop could have been describing a severe case of measles, a disease with which smallpox was often confused in ancient times. The two diseases weren't clearly distinguished until early in the tenth century. That was when the well-known Muslim physician Rhazes published the results of his observations at the hospital in Baghdad.

Rhazes's complete and accurate description of smallpox symptoms formed the basis of all medical texts dealing with the disease for the next 700 years. But Rhazes—along with other physicians of the time—had no idea what caused the disease or how to treat it.

If the patient's eyes were affected, Rhazes advised that a lotion be applied that contained, among other things, "the dung of sparrows, starlings, and mice." However, he also urged the physician "to look carefully and frequently into the eye, and if it be painful and red, then omit this treatment for some days."

Since smallpox patients suffered from high temperatures and burning sensations, Rhazes prescribed bleeding to cool the blood. He also recommended what he called "sweat therapy" to help rid the patient's system of excess humors. (Like the physicians who treated victims of the Black Death, Rhazes had studied and accepted Galen's theory of humors.)

Rhazes also believed that red objects were helpful in treating smallpox patients. It's hard to know where this notion originated. Perhaps it came from the fact that the color red had always been associated with fire and heat. At any rate, Rhazes planted the idea, and later Muslim physicians took it a step further. In the eleventh century, Avicenna advised that a smallpox patient be "wrapped in a woolen cloth of a red color, so that the sight of the red cloth may move the blood to the patient's exterior and hold it there in a moderate heat."

Many European doctors read the works of Rhazes and Avicenna and adopted their recommendations of the so-called "red treatment." When England's young Prince John (a son of Edward II) fell ill with smallpox in 1314, his doctors not only covered him with red blankets and hung red curtains around his bed, but also made him suck the juice of a red pomegranate and gargle with red mulberry wine.

The prince survived, although probably not because of the "red treatment." Hundreds of other people in England died, however, in the smallpox epidemics that swept across the British Isles and western Europe during the 1300s.

Historians think the Crusades were responsible for these epidemics. Between the eleventh and fourteenth centuries, thousands of European Christians journeyed eastward to the Holy Land, where smallpox had long been endemic. There the Christians waged the series of wars known as the Crusades in an attempt to recover the Holy Land from the Muslims. When the Crusaders returned home to Europe, they may well have brought lethal new strains of the smallpox virus with them.

A SCOURGE OF CHILDREN

Unlike the bubonic plague, which spread by a third party—namely, a flea from a plague-ridden rat—smallpox was almost always transmitted directly from one person to another. And this could happen only when the person was actively sick or immediately after death, as possibly was the case with Ramses V.

Moreover, if an infected person survived the disease, he or she would be immune from another attack, usually for life. A person who was immune could not transmit the disease either.

Once smallpox entered a community, it never entirely left it. After a major epidemic, however, there was usually a lull during which only a few scattered cases were reported. Why? Because those who had survived the previous epidemic were immune to the disease, and the number of people who had never been exposed to it was still small.

Eventually, as more and more children were born, a reservoir of susceptible people would build up again. Then one or two cases could spread quickly through the community, and a new smallpox epidemic would occur. Paris, France, was struck by such an epidemic in 1438. Before it ran its course, 50,000 people reportedly died, the majority of them children under the age of twelve.

The death toll could be even more devastating if smallpox hit a people who had never experienced the disease before. That's what happened when European explorers like Christopher Columbus began to voyage to the New World at the end of the fifteenth century. For along with their ships' cargoes of food, weapons, and other supplies, a few of the Europeans carried with them the deadly smallpox virus.

CHAPTER SEVEN

SMALLPOX CONQUERS THE NEW WORLD

When Christopher Columbus landed on the Caribbean island the Spaniards called Hispaniola, he was welcomed by representatives of the Taino people. More than a million Tainos could be found on Hispaniola in 1492. They lived in large, permanent villages, fished the clear waters of the Caribbean, and harvested abundant crops of beans, maize, and squash.

This pleasant way of life was soon to change for the worse. By 1518, just twenty years after Columbus's arrival in the New World, more than a third of the Tainos were dead. Many had perished while working in the gold-mining camps the Spanish had set up. Others starved because of the disruption of their traditional agriculture. But the majority fell victim to epidemic diseases that they had never been exposed to before and against which they had no defenses. The greatest killer of all was smallpox.

From Hispaniola, the smallpox virus traveled to the neighboring islands of Puerto Rico and Cuba, killing large parts of the native populations on both. Now it was only a matter of time before it struck the mainland somewhere in the Americas.

In 1519, the Spanish soldier and explorer Hernando Cortés sailed from Cuba to Mexico with a band of 550 men. Mexico was home to the powerful Aztec empire, which was rumored to be extremely wealthy. Lured by the tales of gold and other riches, the Spaniards reached the Aztec capital, Tenochtitlán, in early November.

The Aztecs had achieved a high degree of skill in architecture and engineering. Their capital—now the site of Mexico City—was built on a series of islands in the middle of a large lake. As Cortés and his men advanced toward the city on a broad causeway, they looked ahead in wonder. "We were all struck with amazement by the towers and temples," wrote one of Cortés's lieutenants. "Some of us kept asking ourselves whether what we saw was not all a dream."

The Aztecs and their emperor, Montezuma, thought the Spaniards were descendants of the Aztec god Quetzalcoatl and received them with respect. Cortés, seeing a unique opportunity, put Montezuma under house arrest and demanded a treasure in gold. The Aztec nobles complied with the Spanish demand, and Cortés attempted to rule the empire through the captive Montezuma.

Up to this point, smallpox and other epidemic diseases had played no part in the Spanish assault on the Aztec empire. Then, in the spring of 1520, another band of Spanish soldiers, this one led by Pánfilo de Narváez, landed on the eastern coast of Mexico. In one of Narváez's ships, according to a priest who wrote an account of the expedition, "there was a black African stricken with smallpox, a disease which had never been seen here before."

The African was probably a slave. Starting around 1510, the Spanish had begun to transport slaves from Africa to the New World. The Africans replaced the dying Tainos as laborers in the gold mines and sugar-cane plantations the Spanish had established on Hispaniola and other Caribbean islands. They also served on occasion in Spanish military expeditions, like the one under the leadership of Pánfilo de Narváez.

When Cortés heard that another Spanish force had landed on the coast, he assembled part of his army, left Tenochtitlán, and moved to put down his rival. Cortés succeeded in doing so, but during the struggle the infected African must have given smallpox to a vulnerable soldier in Cortés's army.

While Cortés was away, the Aztecs rose up in revolt against the Spaniards he had left behind in Tenochtitlán. Cortés raced back to the capital to rescue his colleagues, but the Aztec army still outnumbered the combined Spanish force by more than a hundred to one. Under cover of night, Cortés and his men were forced to flee Tenochtitlán over a bridge composed of abandoned baggage and the bodies of dead soldiers.

It seemed like a total defeat for the Spaniards, but without knowing it, they had left a secret weapon behind. One of the dead Spanish soldiers had smallpox. When the Aztecs examined his body in a search for valuables, they accidentally inhaled the deadly smallpox virus that remained on the soldier's corpse and clothing.

Within a few weeks, the disease spread throughout Tenochtitlán, killing at least a fourth of the capital's population. It claimed huge numbers of the Aztec army and the emperor himself. Then the epidemic widened out to the surrounding countryside. A Spanish priest described its terrible effects there: "As the Indians [of Mexico] did not know the remedy of the disease . . . they died in heaps, like bedbugs. In many places it happened that everyone in a house died and, as it was impossible to bury the great number of dead, they pulled down the houses over them so that their homes became their tombs."

In the meantime, Cortés regrouped his forces and prepared to attack Tenochtitlán again. He returned in August 1521 and easily defeated the weakened Aztec army. After the battle, the Spanish found so many dead lying about the city—victims of smallpox, not the fighting—that they claimed they could not walk through the streets without stepping on bodies. The mighty Aztec empire had been brought low by disease, and it would never rise again.

THE FATE OF THE INCAS

Neither the Spaniards nor smallpox halted their march with the conquest of Mexico. In fact, the disease often traveled faster than the Spanish soldiers. From Mexico, it spread down through Central America and in less than ten years reached the vast empire of the Incas.

At its peak, the Incan empire extended for more than two thousand miles down the western coast of South America. Its capital was Cuzco, located high in the Andes Mountains in what is today Peru. From Cuzco, an elaborate system of roads connected the various parts of the empire and enabled the Incan emperor—who was known as the "Son of the Sun"—to maintain control over his sprawling domain.

When a smallpox epidemic struck Cuzco in 1527, the emperor was on a trip to the city of Quito in the northern part of the empire. Runners from the capital informed him that the disease had already killed his brother, his sister, his uncle, and many other relatives.

The emperor hurried back toward Cuzco but fell ill himself on the way. Taken to one of his palaces, he realized he was dying. He summoned his followers and said, "My father the Sun is calling me. I shall go now to rest at his side."

The emperor then ordered his followers to seal him with stones inside the palace and leave him to die unattended. After eight days, the followers went in, removed his dead body, embalmed it, dressed it in his finest armor, and carried it on their shoulders to Cuzco for burial. Crowds of people lined the roads to pay their last respects to the emperor as his remains passed by.

Historians estimate that 100,000 people died in Quito alone during the smallpox epidemic that killed the Incan emperor. Among them were some of the nation's highest military and political leaders, including the emperor's chosen successor. Civil war broke out between the ruler's two surviving sons. After a long, bloody conflict, the son named Atahualpa finally emerged victorious in 1532. His triumph was short-lived, however, for at almost the same time the Spanish under Francisco Pizarro invaded the empire.

Pizarro, like Cortés in Mexico, commanded an army of fewer than 600 soldiers and missionaries. But the Spanish had the advantage of guns, artillery, and horses, none of which were known to the Incas. (An ancestor of the modern horse did once roam the plains of the Americas, but it had become extinct thousands of years before the arrival of the Spanish.)

Through trickery, Pizarro captured the new emperor, Atahualpa, and had him put to death. Then Pizarro and his small band of Spaniards assumed control of the mighty Incan empire. At once they began to exploit its riches, especially the large deposits of gold, silver, and other precious metals.

The Incas might still have regrouped their forces and driven out the invaders. But before they could do so, they were hit by another smallpox epidemic, this one probably brought by the Spanish. As a missionary close to Pizarro commented, "The Indians die so easily that the bare look and smell of a Spaniard causes them to give up the ghost."

Another witness to the epidemic left a description of its effects that sounds remarkably like accounts of the Black Death: "[The Incas] died by the scores and hundreds. Villages were depopulated. Corpses were scattered over the fields or piled up in the houses or huts. . . . The fields were uncultivated; the herds were untended; and the workshops and mines were without laborers. . . . The price of food rose to such an extent that many persons found it beyond their reach. They escaped the foul disease, only to be wasted by famine."

Some sympathetic Spaniards urged their king to take steps to help the Incas before they all died out. But there was little the king in faraway Spain could do, even if he had wanted to. By the end of the sixteenth century, disease and warfare had reduced the native population of the Incan empire to less than a quarter of its former size.

Smallpox also accompanied the Portuguese when they began to establish colonies in Brazil in the 1500s. Jesuit missionaries made the situation worse by herding the native Indians into settlements where they would be baptized and live as Christians. The crowded conditions in the settlements only helped to spread smallpox among the defenseless Indians.

Like European doctors at the time, the missionaries practiced bleeding as a treatment for smallpox. In their attempts to fend off the disease, they also staged long religious processions in which all the marchers prayed together loudly. However, the processions probably made person-to-person transmission that much easier.

By the middle of the seventeenth century, more than 100,000 Indians were huddled around ten Jesuit missions in Brazil. A smallpox epidemic in 1660 carried off an estimated 44,000 Indians, and another in 1669 killed 20,000 more. As their converts died, the Jesuits responded by rounding up fresh recruits from the remote interior of the country. John Hemming, an Englishman who wrote about the conquest of the Brazilian Indians, commented: "Some of the Jesuits may have believed that it was better for Indians to be baptized but dead than heathen but alive and free."

ON TO NORTH AMERICA

Before 1600, smallpox was unknown among the 20 million or so Native Americans who lived in what are today the United States and Canada. But these Americans would soon suffer the same fate that befell the Indians of Latin America. Beginning in the early 1600s, Great Britain, France, and Holland established permanent settlements in North America. And with the Europeans came smallpox and other contagious diseases that the Native Americans had never encountered before.

In 1633, a smallpox epidemic struck the Native Americans living near the Plymouth Colony in Massachusetts. Increase Mather, one of Boston's leading Puritan clergymen and an early president of Harvard college, thought the epidemic indicated that God was on the colonists' side. Mather wrote:

"The Indians began to be quarrelsome concerning the bounds of the land they had sold to the English; but God ended the controversy by sending the smallpox amongst the Indians at Saugust, who were before that time exceeding numerous. Whole towns of them were swept away, in some of them not so much as one Soul escaping the destruction."

The virus soon traveled inland. When it reached the Huron tribe north of Lake Ontario in 1636, "terror was universal," according to the account of a French missionary. "The contagion increased as autumn advanced; and when winter came . . . its ravages were appalling. The season of Huron festivity was turned to a season of mourning."

The Iroquois, who lived in upper New York State and Canada, were also hit hard by smallpox. The governor of Canada described an outbreak among them in 1679: "The small pox desolates them to such a degree, that they think no longer of meeting nor of wars, but only of bewailing the dead, of whom there is already an immense number."

Although they weren't affected as severely as the native population, the North American colonists suffered from smallpox, too. Unlike the situation in Europe, where the disease was always present to a greater or lesser degree in the larger cities, it died out between epidemics in the smaller cities of the American colonies. This only made its impact more shocking when a new epidemic struck.

Boston alone had to withstand six major smallpox

epidemics between 1636 and 1698. Rather than risk infection, those who could left the city at the start of an epidemic—just as city dwellers threatened by the bubonic plague had done three centuries earlier in Europe.

The worst epidemic yet hit Boston in the late spring of 1721. It was brought to the city by two infected sailors on a ship from the West Indies. Health officials quarantined the sailors in a house near the docks, but the disease spread anyway. As Cotton Mather wrote in his diary, "The grievous calamity of smallpox has now entered the town."

Mather, the son of Increase Mather, was pastor of Boston's North Church. A graduate of Harvard, he had thought of becoming a doctor before entering the ministry, and had long been interested in science. His scientific articles on American plants, birds, and snakes had circulated in England and won him a membership in the exclusive Royal Society.

Now, faced with a new smallpox epidemic in Boston, Mather remembered a letter he had read some years before in the journal of the Royal Society. The letter described a method of preventing smallpox that country people in Turkey had used with great success. The method was called inoculation.

CHAPTER EIGHT

INOCULATION: GODSEND OR DANGER?

The theory behind inoculation was not new. For centuries, Chinese doctors had conferred immunity on people by blowing dust from the scabs of smallpox patients up the nostrils of the healthy. This often produced a mild infection in the patient, but from then on he or she was immune to any further attacks of the disease.

Country people in eastern Europe also practiced a similar form of immunization, which they called *buying the smallpox*. But most Europeans and Americans had never heard of the practice until the journal of the Royal Society published the letter that Cotton Mather read. It told how inoculation had been used to help stem an outbreak of smallpox that had struck the city of Constantinople (now Istanbul, Turkey) in 1706.

Soon after the letter appeared, an unusual English-

woman, Lady Mary Wortley Montagu, began to promote the idea of inoculation. Lady Mary, a talented
poet and tireless letter writer, was the wife of the
British ambassador to Constantinople, then the capital
of the Ottoman Empire. She had strong personal reasons for being concerned about smallpox. Her younger
brother had died of the disease, and she herself had
survived a severe attack that left her without eyelashes
and with a badly pockmarked face. She wrote a poem
about the experience that began:

> In tears, surrounded by friends I lay,
> Mask'd o'er and trembling at the sight of day.

In Constantinople, Lady Mary heard of inoculation and described the practice in a letter to a friend in
London. "The smallpox, so fatal, and so general
amongst us, is here entirely harmless, by the invention
of *ingrafting*, which is the term they give it. There is a
set of old women who make it their business to
perform the operation, every autumn in the month of
September, when the great heat is abated."

Unlike the Chinese, the old women of Constantinople scratched the recipient's upper arm and injected the powdered scabs from a smallpox patient in
the scratch rather than up the nostrils. As in China, the
inoculation caused a mild case of smallpox to develop.
Once the person recovered, however, he or she would

usually be safe from the disease forever.

"Every year thousands undergo this operation," Lady Mary went on. "There is no example of anyone that had died in it: and you may believe I am well satisfied of the safety of this experiment, since I intend to try it on my dear little son."

In 1718, without her husband's knowledge, Lady Mary had her five-year-old son inoculated by an old Greek woman. Working alongside the woman was the embassy physician, Charles Maitland. The boy came through the procedure with no ill effects whatsoever. A week later, Lady Mary told her husband about the inoculation, assuring him that their son was "at this time singing and playing and very impatient for his supper."

The Montagu family returned to London a year later, and in 1721 a new smallpox epidemic hit the city. This time Lady Mary decided to have her four-year-old daughter inoculated against the disease. Dr. Maitland performed the operation, which was reported in the newspapers. It was the first professional inoculation to be done in England, and was hailed as a complete success.

Among those who read the reports were members of the British royal family, including Princess Caroline, wife of the Prince of Wales (the future King George II). She had almost lost one of her daughters to smallpox and wanted to have both girls inoculated.

But some British doctors were strongly opposed to

the notion. One, Dr. William Wagstaffe, wrote: "Posterity will scarcely be brought to believe that a method practiced only by a few *Ignorant Women*, amongst an illiterate and unthinking people, should on a sudden, and upon slender experience, so far obtain in one of the most Learned and Polite Nations in the World as to be received into the *Royal Palace.*"

To overcome the opposition, Princess Caroline arranged to have Dr. Maitland inoculate six condemned prisoners at Newgate Prison while the king's physicians looked on. All the prisoners survived the inoculation and were granted their freedom as a reward. Then, to be doubly sure, the Princess ordered the inoculation of all the orphans in London's St. James Parish. Only when she saw that the orphans, too, had come through the operation unharmed did the Princess allow her own two daughters to be inoculated by Dr. Maitland. Their recovery put the royal seal of approval on the procedure.

In spite of this, inoculation was still not widely practiced in Great Britain. Some people feared that those who had recently been inoculated and were experiencing a mild case of the disease would spread it to susceptible persons in the community. Others objected to the procedure on religious grounds. Like the people of an earlier age who believed the Black Death was the will of God, they wondered whether inoculating someone with smallpox, or permitting themselves to be inoculated, would be seen as interfering with God's intentions. Perhaps He would be angry with them.

Some British clergymen played on these worries. In a sermon delivered in 1722, the Rev. Edmund Massey cited Job, who suffered terribly in the Old Testament but never challenged God's tests of him. "The fear of disease is a happy restraint to men," Massey said. "If men were more healthy, 'tis a great chance they would be less righteous. Let the Atheist and the Scoffer inoculate. Their hope is in and for only this life. Let the rest of us bless God for the Afflictions He sends among us, and grant us patience under them."

The resistance to inoculation only made Lady Mary Wortley Montagu work harder to win acceptance for it. She visited patients recovering from the procedure and encouraged more doctors to perform inoculations. She also wrote letters to newspapers advocating the practice. "I shall sell no drugs, nor take no fees, could I persuade people of the safety and reasonableness of this easy operation," she said in one letter. " 'Tis no way my interest . . . to convince the world of their errors; that is, I shall get nothing by it but the private satisfaction of having done good to mankind. . . ."

Thanks to the efforts of Lady Mary and other supporters, by 1723 inoculations were being performed successfully on more and more English patients. Lady Mary must have felt vindicated. She wrote to her sister,

"I know nobody that has repented the operation, though it has been very troublesome to some fools, who had rather be sick by their doctor's prescriptions than in health because of an inoculation."

UPROAR IN BOSTON

Meanwhile, in the Massachusetts Colony, Cotton Mather had been waging his own campaign to promote inoculation. In June 1721, he stood in his pulpit and urged Boston's physicians to adopt inoculation as a means of halting the smallpox epidemic that was sweeping the city.

Only one of Boston's ten physicians, Dr. Zabdiel Boylston, responded to Mather's call. Using a sharp toothpick and a quill, Boylston inoculated his six-year-old son, Thomas, and two African-American slaves with pus from a smallpox patient. All three developed mild infections, which left them immune afterward.

Many of Boston's other physicians and ministers, as well as a large part of the populace, were outraged that Boylston had deliberately infected three people with smallpox. Public meetings were held at which inoculation was denounced as a dangerous practice.

As in England, the physicians expressed the fear that patients who had been inoculated would infect others while they were getting over the disease. The Boston ministers sincerely believed that using inoculations to prevent smallpox would be interfering with God's will.

Tensions mounted to such a pitch that Dr. Boylston had to hide in his house for two weeks after an angry crowd threatened to drag him out and hang him. Someone threw a homemade grenade into Cotton Mather's house, but it failed to explode. Attached to the grenade was a note that read, "Cotton Mather, you dog. Damn you! I'll inoculate you with this, and a pox to you!"

As the months passed, the mood of the city calmed down somewhat. Dr. Boylston resumed his inoculations and two other doctors joined him in performing them. Cotton Mather answered the charges of other ministers by preaching that God must be in favor of inoculation since it saved lives. But there were still loud rumblings of protest against the activities of both men.

The controversy surrounding inoculation was brought home to Mather in a very personal way when his son Samuel asked that he be inoculated. Samuel's roommate at Harvard College had died painfully of smallpox, and Samuel feared he might contract the disease.

Cotton Mather didn't know what to do. If he refused to let his beloved son be inoculated, and Samuel died of the disease, how could Mather forgive himself? "On the other hand," Mather wrote, "our People . . . will go on with infinite Prejudices against me and my

Ministry, if I suffer this Operation upon the child."

In the end, Mather's feelings for his son out-weighed his worries about his reputation, and Samuel was inoculated by Dr. Boylston. The young man made a speedy recovery, and proved to be a wonderful living advertisement for the inoculation process.

When the smallpox epidemic in Boston finally came to an end in the spring of 1722, it was revealed that Dr. Boylston and his two colleagues had inoculated 280 patients. Only six of them died from the disease—a little more than two percent. On the other side, out of a preepidemic population of 11,000, more than 5800 uninoculated Bostonians had come down with smallpox, and 844—or fifteen percent—had died. This seemed to prove beyond a doubt the benefits of inoculation.

After its successful use in Boston, inoculation was employed to help fight smallpox epidemics in Philadel-phia, New York City, and Charleston, South Carolina, during the 1730s. Nowhere did the practice generate the kind of controversy it had aroused in Boston.

Benjamin Franklin, then the editor of the *Pennsyl-vania Gazette*, promoted inoculation in Philadelphia, and the city became a center for the treatment. Patients from all the American colonies and the West Indies, too, traveled to Philadelphia to be inoculated.

The well-to-do often made inoculation into a social occasion. Entire families, or groups of good friends, would arrange to be inoculated together and share the one or two weeks of required isolation afterward. Abigail Adams took her four children to the home of an aunt in Boston for their inoculations. There they recuperated together while her husband, John Adams—who was to become the second President of the United States—attended the First Continental Congress in Philadelphia.

Because inoculation was quite an expensive procedure, Benjamin Franklin and others urged that ways be found to make it available to the poor as well as the rich. Responding to their call, Philadelphia established the Society for the Inoculation of the Poor in 1774. Through the efforts of the Society and similar organizations elsewhere, the death rate from smallpox dropped sharply in the cities along the eastern seaboard during the later years of the eighteenth century.

One group of Americans was overlooked as the colonies moved to adopt inoculation on a wider scale. These were the members of the Native American tribes who lived in the vast region beyond the colonies' western boundaries. In fact, far from trying to control smallpox among Native Americans, the settlers sometimes plotted to spread the disease among them.

The most notorious example of this occurred in 1763. That was when Sir Jeffrey Amherst, commander-in-chief of British forces in North America, became alarmed by Native American attacks on his troops as the British moved westward.

In a letter to one of his colonels, Amherst made a drastic suggestion: "Could it not be contrived to send the smallpox among these . . . tribes of Indians? We must on this occasion use every stratagem in our power to reduce them."

The colonel replied: "I will try to inoculate [infect] the Indians with some blankets that may fall in their hands, and take care not to get the disease myself."

Amherst was all in favor of the colonel's plan. "You will do well to try to infect the Indians by means of blankets," he wrote, "as well as to try every other method that can serve to extirpate this execrable race."

Shortly thereafter, the colonel invited two Native American chiefs to the British camp. He told the chiefs he wanted to resolve the tense military situation that existed between the two groups. An officer who was present revealed the true purpose of the meeting in his diary. "Out of our regard for [the chiefs] we gave them two blankets and handkerchiefs out of the smallpox hospital. I hope they will have the desired effect."

It is not known for certain whether they did or not. But Native American resistance to the British and American forces weakened noticeably in the next few months, and it may well have been due to the colonel's poisonous "gift."

SMALLPOX IN THE AMERICAN REVOLUTION

During the American Revolution, which began in 1775, smallpox was a bigger problem for the American army than it was for the British. More British soldiers had had the disease, naturally or through inoculation, and thus more of them were immune to it.

The American leader, General George Washington, was well aware of the damage smallpox could do. He himself had survived an attack while visiting his brother on the island of Barbados in 1751, but it had left his face pockmarked. Now, not wanting to lose any of his soldiers to the disease, General Washington moved cautiously.

When the British gave up Boston in 1776, Washington at first would let only a thousand American soldiers who had already had smallpox enter the city. He was worried that his other soldiers might contract the disease from contaminated objects—sheets, towels, etc.—that the British had left behind.

At first Washington and the other American commanders were hesitant to launch a major campaign to inoculate American soldiers. They feared the soldiers would spread the disease to their fellows while they were in the contagious phase. Eventually, Washington changed his mind about mass inoculations. He decided the risk was worth it if the health of most of his men could be preserved. "I would fain hope," Washington wrote, "that in a short space of time we shall have an army not subject to this, the greatest of all calamities that can befall it."

From all the evidence, Washington's inoculation policy worked. Although the American army suffered many setbacks, it was never laid low by a major smallpox epidemic. And it finally triumphed over the British at the battle of Yorktown, Virginia, in 1781.

As inoculation became more commonplace in Europe and America, the death rate from smallpox continued to decline. Epidemics broke out occasionally, however, hitting large, crowded cities like London especially hard. The majority of the victims were young, poor children who had not been inoculated. In some English cities, such as Manchester and Birmingham, nine of every ten persons who died of smallpox were under five years old.

A French doctor in the late 1700s estimated that, despite the widespread use of inoculation, one fourth of the human race was still being killed, blinded, or disfigured for life by smallpox. But a new means of prevention was about to be discovered, one that would bring the disease under control at last. This was vaccination.

CHAPTER NINE

DR. JENNER'S MARVELOUS VACCINE

When Edward Jenner was eight years old, he had a painful experience that he never forgot. Later, it helped inspire him to seek a safer and more efficient means of preventing smallpox.

Edward was the younger son of the rector of a little church in Berkeley, in the western English county of Gloucestershire. Both his parents died when Edward was five, and his older brother, Stephen—a minister like their father—took charge of Edward's upbringing.

Stephen was well-read and open to new scientific ideas like inoculation. So when a smallpox epidemic broke out in Gloucestershire in 1757, Stephen arranged to have his younger brother inoculated with a number of other children.

The inoculations were to be administered by a local pharmacist in a stable that he owned. First, though, the man bled Edward and the other children repeatedly over a period of six weeks—a procedure that dated to the time of the Black Death and even earlier. The pharmacist also gave the children large doses of laxatives to empty their stomachs.

At last the day for the inoculations arrived. Edward, like the other children, lay on a table while the pharmacist scratched his left arm with the tip of a knife, placed the dried scab from a smallpox victim over the cuts, and bandaged the arm. Edward could not go home afterward. Instead, he and the other children were forced to stay in the stable until the pharmacist judged they were no longer contagious.

After about a week, Edward, like most of the others in the stable, came down with a mild case of smallpox. His temperature soared and the characteristic rash appeared on his skin. Within three days, though, his temperature went down and the rash gradually faded away.

Shortly thereafter, the pharmacist told Edward he could go home to his brother. As he unlocked the stable door, the man clapped Edward on the shoulder and said he was now immune to any future attack of smallpox. But it took the boy almost a month to recover fully from the disease and the bleeding and purging that had preceded it.

From early childhood, Edward had shown an interest

in nature and science. Sensing this, his brother Stephen arranged for him to become, at age thirteen, an apprentice to a physician in a nearby town. It was while helping Dr. Daniel Ludlow with his work that Edward first heard farm people say that they could not get smallpox because they had already had the cowpox.

Cowpox, a relatively mild disease of cattle, usually caused a few blisters on the udders of infected cows. Milkmaids and other farm workers could acquire the disease when they milked sick animals. Painful sores broke out on their hands and sometimes left scars, but the disease soon passed and—unlike smallpox—was not fatal.

Young Jenner was intrigued by the stories he heard about cowpox providing its human victims with an immunity to smallpox. But Dr. Ludlow pooh-poohed them, saying there was no evidence of a connection between the two diseases.

When Edward had learned all he could locally, his brother sent him to London to study medicine with a prominent doctor there. Edward did so well that his teacher offered him a permanent position, but Edward decided he would rather return to his hometown of Berkeley to practice. In 1773 he converted a room in his brother's house into an office and set himself up as the town's only physician.

A new smallpox epidemic struck Gloucestershire in

1778. As Jenner traveled around the county giving in-oculations, he was often reminded of the stories about cowpox that he had heard as a boy. Many farmworkers whom Jenner approached flatly refused to be inoculated. They told him they had already had the cowpox, and that it prevented smallpox. So there was no need to give them inoculations.

The farmworkers' stubborn resistance made Jenner think they might be right. Over the next several years, he spent much time studying cowpox. He went to one dairy farm after another, looking for cases of the disease. Some of the farmers welcomed him; others thought he was odd or maybe even a little crazy.

During his investigations, Jenner discovered that cowpox protected a person against smallpox only if he or she caught the disease when it was at its height in the infected animal. A day or two earlier or later, and the case of cowpox that resulted would be too weak to provide immunity.

He also got the idea that it might be possible, as with smallpox, to infect a person with a mild case of cowpox by inoculation. He thought this could be done first with disease-laden matter from a cow. Then matter from a sore on the infected person could be used to inoculate other humans. But it wasn't until 1796 that he was able to test his theories.

In May of that year, a local milkmaid named Sarah

Nelmes cut her finger on a thorn just before milking a cow that was suffering from cowpox. Soon, a large, pus-filled sore appeared on Sarah's finger, followed by two smaller ones on her wrist.

The young woman went to Dr. Jenner for treatment, and he realized that her infection was nearing its peak. This was the chance he had been waiting for. After reassuring Sarah that she would recover, he asked her to come back in a few days, when he estimated the cowpox sores would be at their worst.

In the meantime, Dr. Jenner sought out an eight-year-old boy, James Phipps, who had never had either cowpox or smallpox. Although he could not guarantee the boy's safety, Jenner obtained the permission of James's parents to conduct an experiment on their son.

When Sarah returned to Jenner's office, James Phipps was waiting there with the doctor. First Jenner took some pus from the sore on Sarah's finger. Then, after making two small scratches on James's left arm, the doctor inserted the pus in the cuts. Afterward, he sent both James and Sarah home. There was no need for the boy to be isolated, as Jenner once had been, since cowpox could not be transmitted from one human being to another.

Jenner checked on James's condition every day. "On the ninth day," the doctor wrote, "he became a little chilly, lost his appetite, and had a headache. . . . [He] spent the night with some degree of restlessness, but on the day following he was perfectly well."

Now came the risky part of the experiment. On July 1, Jenner repeated the inoculation procedure on James Phipps, this time with matter from a smallpox patient. How would James react? Jenner thought the earlier cowpox infection would render the boy immune to the smallpox, but he couldn't be sure.

Happily, Jenner was proved right. On July 19, he reported on the results of the experiment in a letter to a friend: ". . . But now listen to the most delightful part of my story. The Boy has since been inoculated for the Smallpox which as I ventured to predict produced no [ill] effects [whatsoever]. I shall now pursue my Experiments with redoubled ardor."

The following year Jenner submitted a brief article to the Royal Society describing his experiment on James Phipps. However, it was returned to him with a note from the editors saying they found his evidence too thin. They also thought it most unlikely that anyone would believe cowpox could be used to prevent smallpox.

Jenner did not let this rejection from the Society stop him. He continued his experiments and, in 1798, inoculated five more children with cowpox. Later he followed up by inoculating three of the children with smallpox, and none of them became ill.

Jenner was now more convinced than ever that his theories were correct. He wrote a pamphlet summarizing his findings, and this time he published it himself instead of trying to go through the Royal Society. In the pamphlet, Jenner called the matter he had taken from the cowpox sore a *vaccine*, from the Latin for *obtained from a cow*. The process itself he called *vaccination*, to distinguish it from inoculation. Now the word *vaccination* is used for any immunization process that protects against a particular disease, and vaccines are obtained from many different sources.

Other English doctors read Jenner's pamphlet and conducted successful experiments of their own. Many of them published accounts that lent further support to his theories. Edward Jenner was elated. In a letter to a colleague, he predicted that "the annihilation of smallpox—the most dreadful scourge of the human race—will be the final result of [vaccination]."

The good news about vaccination traveled far beyond the borders of England. Within a few years, Jenner's pamphlet had been translated into German, French, Spanish, Dutch, and Italian. Copies of the English edition were shipped across the Atlantic to the newly independent United States.

In many places, vaccination soon replaced inoculation as the preferred method of preventing smallpox. Vaccination was simpler and cheaper than the earlier treatment, since patients did not have to remain isolated for one or two weeks after being vaccinated. It was safer, too, because cowpox was a much less severe disease.

Not everyone approved of vaccination, however. A British surgeon named John Birch feared it would eliminate a disease that he called "a merciful means of reducing the country's poor population." Some religious leaders opposed vaccination on the familiar ground that it interfered with God's will. But many other ministers and priests endorsed the practice. In Geneva, Switzerland, one minister even permitted a doctor to hand out literature promoting vaccination when parents brought their babies to be baptized.

VACCINATIONS AND EPIDEMICS

Dr. Benjamin Waterhouse did more than any other individual to spread the word about vaccination in the United States. Waterhouse was a Quaker who had studied medicine in England, Scotland, and Holland before returning to Newport, Rhode Island, to set up a practice in 1781. English friends sent him copies of Jenner's writings on the cowpox vaccine.

Dr. Waterhouse recognized the importance of Jenner's discoveries and gave a talk about them at a meeting of the American Academy of Arts and Sciences. Then Waterhouse proceeded to put Jenner's theories to the test by vaccinating his own five-year-old son,

David, and six other members of his household. These were the first vaccinations performed in the United States.

Later, Dr. Waterhouse inoculated David and the others with smallpox, and all of them resisted infection. As with James Phipps in England, vaccination had made them immune to the disease.

Waterhouse performed more vaccinations in New England and published accounts of the results. In 1801, he wrote to President Thomas Jefferson, asking his help in promoting vaccination throughout the country. Jefferson wrote back: "I had before attended to your publications on the subject in the newspapers, and took much interest in the result of the experiments you were making. Every friend of humanity must look with pleasure on this discovery [vaccination], by which one more evil is withdrawn from the condition of man."

With Jefferson's backing, vaccination was introduced in Washington, Baltimore, Philadelphia, and New York City. Jefferson also explained the new preventive measure to a group of Native Americans who had gathered in Washington. The President brought in a doctor to vaccinate the tribesmen and gave them a supply of vaccine to take home, along with instructions on how to use it.

Many Native Americans were suspicious of vaccination, however. George Catlin, an artist who studied and painted the tribes of the Midwest, suggested why Native Americans felt this way. "They see the white men urging the operation [vaccination] so earnestly they decide it must be some new . . . trick of the pale face by which they hope to gain some new advantage over them."

Their suspicions had fatal consequences for several tribes when two great smallpox epidemics swept the Midwest. The first struck the region in 1801–2 and the second between 1836 and 1840.

Both epidemics were accidentally triggered by white traders as they journeyed up the Missouri River by boat. It took only one or two infected crewmen to spread the disease among thousands of Native Americans living along the river. Like the Aztecs in Mexico, the Incas in Peru, and their own fellows in the eastern United States, these peoples had never been exposed to smallpox before and had no defenses against it.

The second epidemic lasted much longer than the first and claimed far more lives. It raged across vast areas of the West and virtually wiped out an entire tribe, the Mandans, who lived in what is now North Dakota.

The Mandan population numbered about two thousand men, women, and children when an American Fur Company steamboat approached their settlement on the bank of the Missouri in June 1837. The steamboat captain knew that two of his sailors were ill with smallpox, but that didn't prevent him from stopping at the settlement to trade. The tribal chiefs came on board to welcome the captain and get a preview of his wares. They were infected unintentionally by the sick sailors, and carried the disease back to their own people. Within days, countless Mandans fell ill.

"There was but one continual crying and howling and praying to the Great Spirit for his protection," George Catlin wrote later in his journal. Catlin was not present in the Mandan village during the epidemic, but heard what happened there from a white trader stationed at nearby Fort Clark.

"Nobody thought of burying the dead," Catlin went on. "Whole families together were left in horrid and loathsome piles in their own wigwams, with a few buffalo robes thrown over them, there to decay, and be devoured by their own dogs."

The disease spread to other tribes in the same epidemic, among them the Blackfeet, Cheyennes, and Crows. Major Joshua Pilcher, then the Superintendent of Indian Affairs at St. Louis, estimated that at least 25,000 members of these tribes died within four or five months.

As for the Mandans, only thirty or forty of the original two thousand survived the epidemic. Dazed and grief-stricken, they were enslaved by the Riccarees, an enemy tribe living two hundred miles south on the

Missouri. The Riccarees moved up and took possession of the Mandans' village because it was better built than their own.

Although there is no evidence that they were started deliberately, the smallpox epidemics of the early nineteenth century furthered the expansionist goals of the young United States. By weakening the Native American tribes of the Midwest and West, the epidemic made it easier for the United States to lay claim to western land. Meanwhile, new advances were being made throughout the world in the ongoing struggle against the disease. Several of them concerned improvements in the vaccination process.

British doctors realized that vaccinations did not always provide lifelong immunity when some people who had been vaccinated developed mild cases of smallpox a few years later. To counter this tendency, the doctors recommended that the average person be revaccinated every seven to ten years. The new policy was introduced in Great Britain and elsewhere in 1829 and made vaccination an even more reliable safeguard against smallpox.

As time went on, it was found that arm-to-arm vaccination from one human being to another could sometimes be dangerous. If the donor was infected with a disease besides cowpox, he or she might transmit it to the recipient along with the vaccine. This problem was solved when a scientist in Italy discovered a way to produce a steady supply of high-quality vaccine in cattle. Now there was no need for an infected person like Sarah Nelmes to be used as a source of cowpox vaccine.

By the middle of the nineteenth century, vaccination had won acceptance in many parts of the world. Massachusetts passed a law in 1855 requiring that all schoolchildren be vaccinated, and New York and other states soon followed its example. England banned inoculation in 1842 and decreed in 1853 that all its citizens be vaccinated instead.

Not everyone was in favor of these new laws. Some saw them as example of government interference with matters that should be left to individual or family choice. Others were simply afraid of being vaccinated. The English humor magazine *Punch* poked fun at these fears when it published the following poem in 1881. It was patterned on the famous soliloquy "To Be or Not to Be" from Shakespeare's play *Hamlet*.

> To vaccinate or not, that is the question!
> Whether 'tis better for a man to suffer
> The painful pangs and lasting scars of smallpox,
> Or to bare arms before the surgeon's lancet,
> And by being vaccinated, end them. Yes!
> To see the tiny point, and say we end

The chance of many a thousand awful scars
That flesh is heir to—'tis a consummation
Devoutly to be wished. . . .

As the nineteenth century neared its end, more and more people followed the advice of the poem's narrator and got vaccinations. Germany enacted a law requiring all German children to be vaccinated before their second birthday and revaccinated at age twelve. Enforced strictly, the law virtually eliminated smallpox as a public health problem in Germany.

Similar laws in other countries showed equally positive results. Taken together, they made it seem as if Edward Jenner's optimistic prediction would be proved correct. Vaccination might really bring about the annihilation of smallpox.

CHAPTER TEN

THE END OF SMALLPOX?

Starting in the 1890s, one country after another reported that vaccination campaigns had wiped out smallpox within its borders. Sweden was the first, in 1895. Puerto Rico initiated an island-wide effort that eliminated the disease in 1899. It vanished from Great Britain, the Philippine Islands, and the Soviet Union in the 1930s.

The United States moved more slowly to eradicate the disease. Some Americans refused on religious grounds to have themselves or their children vaccinated, while others saw compulsory vaccination as an infringement of their civil rights. This led a highly respected scientist, Dr. C. V. Chapin, to state in 1913 that the United States was "the least vaccinated of any civilized country." But the situation gradually improved, and by the late 1940s the United States, too, was free of smallpox. Then came one last, alarming outbreak of the disease in New York City.

In March 1947, an American businessman who had been working in Mexico City got off a bus in New York feeling ill. Taken to a hospital, he was diagnosed as having acute bronchitis. Only after the man died did his doctors realize that he had actually been suffering from smallpox.

The man had come into contact with a number of people while on the bus and in the hospital, and two of them fell ill with the disease also. The media took up the story, and a smallpox scare ensued. New Yorkers feared the city might be swept by a full-scale epidemic.

City health officials responded by announcing a mass campaign to vaccinate or revaccinate everyone who lived in New York. With the help of the Army and Navy and teams of doctors, the campaign was set in motion. By April 20, just a little more than a month after the businessman fell ill, more than 3,450,000 New Yorkers had been vaccinated and no new cases had been reported in a week. The smallpox scare ended as swiftly as it had begun.

Inspired by success stories like this, and the fact that smallpox had been wiped out in most of the industrial countries, a movement began in the United Nations to rid the entire world of smallpox. Two new advances in vaccination made this goal seem possible for the first time. One was a more efficient needle for mass vaccinations. The other was a way of freeze-drying vaccine so that it would retain its potency for months without refrigeration in almost any climate.

With these tools in hand, the World Health Organization (WHO) of the United Nations adopted an ambitious resolution in 1966. It called for the final eradication of smallpox through the combined efforts of all member nations, and set January 1, 1977, as the deadline for this to be accomplished.

At the time the resolution was passed, forty-four countries were still reporting cases of smallpox, and the disease was endemic in thirty-three of them.

Those involved with the eradication program faced many challenges as they prepared to launch their worldwide campaign. Most crucial was the need to prove that smallpox could be wiped out in poorer countries whose transportation systems, sanitation facilities, and health services all tended to be inadequate.

Ways to overcome these hurdles were discovered out of sheer necessity during the eradication campaign in the west African country of Nigeria. Until then, the standard policy had been to conduct mass vaccinations of entire populations. But when an expected shipment of vaccine failed to arrive in Nigeria, the local advisor, Dr. William Foege, had to make do with the limited supply he already had on hand.

Dr. Foege decided on a new policy that he called "surveillance and containment." Instead of performing mass vaccinations throughout the country, he and his staff waited until an outbreak of smallpox was reported in a particular household or village. Then they traveled to the place and vaccinated only those people in the vicinity who might have been exposed to the disease.

Dr. Foege's policy was so successful in Nigeria that other African eradication teams adopted it. As a result, smallpox was completely eliminated in twenty west and central African countries in less than three and a half years.

The surveillance-and-containment policy was equally successful elsewhere. Brazil—the only country in the Americas where smallpox was still endemic—became free of the disease in 1971. Indonesia reported its last case in January 1972. By the end of 1972, outbreaks of smallpox continued to occur in just six countries—four in Asia, including India, and two in east Africa. A terrible epidemic killed more than 25,000 people in India in the spring of 1974.

Health workers in India had to overcome numerous obstacles as they struggled to bring smallpox under control. Worshippers of the Indian smallpox goddess, Sitala, feared that she would vent her anger on them if they allowed themselves to be vaccinated. The health workers had to convince these believers that the goddess would approve of vaccination.

When necessary, the workers made house-by-house searches for smallpox cases. If they found any, they vaccinated everyone within a three-mile radius of the infected family. In the meantime, the disease victims had to remain isolated in their homes, like victims of the bubonic plague in seventeenth-century London, until they were no longer contagious.

India's beggars, some of them professionals, presented a special problem. The beggars often traveled from village to village, and those infected with smallpox spread the disease as they went. Moreover, sick beggars refused to be isolated, saying they would have no income if they left the streets. So health workers came up with a practical solution to the problem: They offered to provide the beggars with food and shelter until the isolation period was over.

By late 1974, 236 specialists in epidemic diseases from thirty nations were contributing their knowledge and experience to the eradication campaign in India. Working closely with them were thousands of Indian specialists and health workers. As a result of their joint efforts, the number of new smallpox cases declined sharply throughout the country in the early months of 1975. Then came the day all the specialists and health workers had been waiting for. On July 4, 1975, the last person in India to suffer from smallpox was released from an isolation hospital and returned to her home.

Now new cases of smallpox were being reported only in two east African countries, Ethiopia and Somalia. The disease was eliminated in Ethiopia by 1976, but it persisted among the nomadic peoples of Somalia. When an outbreak occurred, these Somalis did not want to be confined in their tiny huts or in large, remote isolation camps run by the government.

Health workers in Somalia came up with a solution to the problem that was similar to the one used with the beggars in India. Special isolation areas were created near nomadic encampments where smallpox had broken out. Each area consisted of a hut of wood and thatch and a surrounding fence made of thorn bushes. Guards were posted at the only gate in the fence to make sure no one entered or left.

A cook was assigned to the area and given better food to prepare for the smallpox sufferers than they were likely to get outside. When the sufferers recovered and were released from isolation, each of them received new clothing, a gift of the World Health Organization.

Once this isolation policy was put into practice, it brought quick results. Victims of the disease were no longer reluctant to be confined, and on November 28, 1977, the last known smallpox sufferer in Somalia left an isolation area and rejoined his family.

TO PRESERVE OR DESTROY?

The World Health Organization did not claim immediate victory in the eradication campaign. Instead it sent observers to countries where smallpox had been endemic to make sure it was really gone. While this search was going on, the disease made one last, deadly appearance in a country where it had long been absent.

In September 1978, a small amount of smallpox virus escaped accidentally from a research laboratory in Birmingham, England. It infected a medical photographer named Janet Parker and her aged mother. The mother survived, but Parker died. So did the head of the laboratory, who felt so guilty about the incident that he took his own life.

A year later, in 1979, the World Health Organization made a long-awaited announcement. The results of its survey were in and the word was that smallpox—the disease that had killed millions of people over more than three thousand years—had been totally eliminated from the Earth.

In light of this happy development, WHO recommended that vaccinations against smallpox be stopped everywhere. The United States and other countries had ceased routine vaccinations of children and travelers in the early 1970s, but the armed forces of several nations, including the United States and the Soviet Union, were still being vaccinated.

Scientists and health workers throughout the world rejoiced at WHO's announcement. At the same time, they remembered what had happened in Birmingham and worried about the stockpiles of smallpox virus that laboratories in many nations possessed. Might the disease come back to frightful life if similar accidents occurred at one or more of these laboratories?

Responding to the scientists' concerns, some nations voluntarily destroyed their stocks of the smallpox virus. Others handed them over to research centers in the United States and the Soviet Union, depending on which superpower they were closer to politically. By the late 1980s only six hundred tiny vials of smallpox virus remained. All of them were frozen in liquid nitrogen and were handled only by scientific workers wearing special protective suits.

The U.S. Centers for Disease Control (CDC) stored four hundred of the vials at a laboratory in Atlanta, Georgia. The other two hundred vials were kept in a special freezer in Moscow, the capital of the Soviet Union, and were watched over by a regiment of army officers.

In 1990 the World Health Organization urged that the last two stocks of smallpox virus be destroyed. The organization, expressing the anxieties of many member nations, feared what would happen if the virus were used in biological warfare or if it somehow got into the hands of terrorists.

First the United States and then the Soviet Union decided to support WHO's position. December 31, 1993, was set as the deadline for the final destruction of the virus stocks, probably by heating them to a very high temperature. By that date, WHO thought, scientists in both countries would have completed their studies of the virus and how it worked.

As the deadline neared, arguments went back and forth in political and scientific circles. On the one hand were those who believed the sooner the virus was destroyed, the better, so that smallpox would never again be a threat to humanity. On the other were the scientists who said they needed more time to study the structure of the virus. They contended that a better understanding of the smallpox virus might provide clues that would help in the struggles against other scourges, such as cancer, inherited genetic diseases, and even some forms of heart disease.

WHO decided in favor of the scientists who wanted the virus's destruction to be delayed. December 31, 1993, came and went and the vials of virus stayed in their closely guarded freezers in Atlanta and Moscow. In June 1994, WHO extended the reprieve for another year, until the end of May 1995. Later in 1994, a ten-member committee of WHO recommended unanimously that the smallpox virus be destroyed once and for all on June 30, 1995.

There were still some scientists who favored preserving the virus, however. They pressured the excutive board of WHO, which failed to approve its own committee's recommendation that the virus be destroyed. Thus the smallpox virus was given at least another one-year stay of execution, until June 1996. And the postponement could be indefinite.

Meanwhile, another deadly virus had captured the world's attention, one for which an effective treatment—let alone eradication—was nowhere in sight. This, of course, was AIDS.

CHAPTER ELEVEN

A MYSTERIOUS NEW DISEASE

In the beginning, and for a long time afterward, the new disease was a complete mystery to medical experts. It surfaced first in the central African nation of Zaire sometime in the mid-1970s.

An early victim of the disease was Dr. Grethe Rask, a surgeon from Denmark who had been working at hospitals in Zaire for over three years. In late 1974, Dr. Rask began to suffer from severe diarrhea. Drugs failed to halt the condition, and the doctor lost a great deal of weight.

At the same time, the lymph glands in Dr. Rask's neck and groin and under her arms all began to swell. Such swelling usually indicates that the glands are fighting an infection, but the woman's doctors were unable to pinpoint the specific infection in her case.

Dr. Rask became so fatigued that she could not

continue working. She went home to Denmark for further treatment, but doctors there were no more successful in solving the mystery of her illness than the African doctors. All they knew was that something had seriously weakened the woman's immune system. Tests revealed that her blood contained very few T cells, a kind of white blood cell that plays a key role in defending the body against disease.

Meanwhile, Dr. Rask developed frightening new symptoms. The interior of her mouth became coated with thick white yeast infections. Other bacterial infections spread through her blood. Suddenly she could not breathe without the aid of bottled oxygen.

Dr. Rask underwent test after test, but her doctors still could not discover what was making her so sick. Thin and exhausted from her struggle, Dr. Grethe Rask died at last on December 12, 1977. She was only forty-seven. An autopsy revealed that her lungs were filled with millions of *Pneumocystis carinii* bacteria—the cause of an unusual form of pneumonia. That explained why she had had such trouble breathing, and it was what had ultimately killed her.

But why *Pneumocystis*? The lung disease had not been diagnosed in humans until 1942, and had been observed only rarely in the years since then. A normally functioning immune system usually held it in check.

"THE GAY CANCER"

If there had been no follow-up cases, Dr. Rask's mysterious illness might have been dismissed as a regrettable one-time event. But a few years later, in 1980, some young men in New York City began to complain of similar symptoms. Health officials noted with interest that the men had one factor in common: They were all homosexual.

Like Grethe Rask, these men often suffered from swollen lymph glands, but biopsies indicated they were not due to lymph cancer. The men's T cell counts had also dropped, like hers, to such dangerously low levels that their bodies could not fend off the various diseases that plagued them. One of these was a seldom-seen skin cancer known as *Kaposi's sarcoma*.

Named for the nineteenth-century Austrian dermatologist who discovered it, Kaposi's sarcoma (KS) is characterized by purplish spots that appear on various parts of the body. It can also invade internal organs such as the lungs. Until the early 1980s, the disease had been confined to a few elderly Jewish and Italian men and to the Bantu people of central Africa, and it was usually not fatal. Now a more aggressive form of Kaposi's sarcoma was attacking young gay men.

As they grew weaker, several of these cancer victims also developed *Pneumocystis carinii* pneumonia (PCP), the rare pneumonia that had killed Grethe

Rask. By the end of 1980, the young gay men, too, were dead. Medical researchers began to suspect there was a link between the two diseases, namely the unknown killer of the body's white T cells. But what was it?

Fresh reports of Kaposi's sarcoma, *Pneumocystis carinii* pneumonia, and other related infections increased dramatically among American gay men throughout 1981. The reports came mainly from New York, San Francisco, and other urban centers with large gay populations.

Because this strange new malady seemed to affect only homosexual men, news stories referred to it as "the gay cancer" or "the gay plague." But the media did not give it much coverage in the beginning. They thought that most of their readers and viewers would not be interested in the health problems of gays. Especially not if their sexual orientation had anything to do with their getting the disease.

From the days of the Puritans in New England, Americans have found it difficult to deal frankly and openly with human sexuality. Same-sex relationships are frowned on particularly. The Roman Catholic Church, Orthodox Judaism, and fundamentalist Protestant groups all condemn the open expression of homosexual feelings, citing passages from the Bible as justification. Many states and cities have laws on their books prohibiting homosexual acts, even in private. Not until 1973 did the American Psychiatric Association remove homosexuality from its list of mental diseases.

The gay liberation movement, the modern phase of which began in 1969 with a riot against police harassment at the Stonewall Inn in New York City, improved the situation somewhat. It spawned slogans like "Gay is good," led to the annual staging of Gay Pride parades in cities across the country, and encouraged a wider discussion of gay issues in the media and elsewhere. But the movement also resulted in excesses on both sides.

As more gay men and women declared themselves by "coming out of the closet" and demanding their civil rights, religious fundamentalists and other conservatives reacted strongly. Groups affirming what they called "family values" accused gays of seeking special privileges. These groups lobbied for new state and local laws that would strictly limit the rights of gays.

For their part, some gay men in the 1970s responded to the new climate of freedom by indulging their sexual impulses without regard to the consequences. The men frequented gay bathhouses, where they engaged in oral and anal sex with strangers. As a result, a large number became infected with sexually transmitted diseases such as syphilis, gonorrhea, and hepatitis B. These diseases could be cured with antibiotics and vaccines, but they seriously weakened their victims' immune systems. Thus many male homosexuals were unusually vulnerable when the mysterious "gay plague" or "gay cancer" attacked their T cells.

Both of those names for the condition soon proved to be inaccurate, however. Reports coming in from around the country indicated that other groups besides gays were being affected. Male heroin addicts showed up in New York City emergency rooms suffering from PCP. A female drug user in New York displayed an extremely low T-cell count for no apparent reason, and so did her newborn child. Haitian male immigrants in Florida and New York fell ill with PCP and other diseases that were infecting gay men, yet the Haitians claimed they were heterosexual.

Hearing these reports, doctors, health officials, and scientists realized the incidents must be connected in some way, but how? Could something in the environment—some poisonous bacterium—be destroying these peoples' immune systems? If so, it should be relatively easy to detect and bring under control. But what if the destruction was caused by an unknown and deadly virus? That possibility was far more alarming.

Then the Centers for Disease Control in Atlanta, Georgia, received a disturbing new report from a doctor in Florida. An elderly male patient with a weakened immune system had contracted *Pneumocystis carinii* pneumonia and died of the disease. The man was not a homosexual and did not inject drugs, but he was a hemophiliac who required special medical treatments. His doctor wondered if those treatments had something to do with the man's getting *Pneumocystis*.

Hemophilia is an inherited disorder that prevents a person's blood from clotting. It is usually transmitted by the mother to her male children only. Small wounds and punctures, which are quickly sealed over by clotted blood in an ordinary individual, can bleed uncontrollably and be life threatening for a hemophiliac. Internal bleeding often fills the spaces around the person's joints and leads to permanent crippling.

Until recently, a hemophiliac could expect to live for only two or three decades, marked by frequent hospital visits for blood transfusions. Then a substance called Factor VIII was developed. Unlike transfusions that merely replace lost blood, Factor VIII contains a clotting factor concentrated from thousands of blood donors. When a hemophiliac receives injections of Factor VIII, his blood is able to clot itself and he can look forward to an almost normal life span.

The elderly Florida hemophiliac who died of *Pneumocystis* organisms had been receiving Factor VIII injections for some time. Was it possible, his doctor asked, that the *Pneumocystis* organisms had been transmitted to him in the clotting substance?

No, responded scientists at the Centers for Disease Control. During its preparation, Factor VIII goes through a filtering process that would screen out the relatively large *Pneumocystis* bacteria. Reassured, the Florida doctor accepted their explanation. But some of the scientists had a troubling second thought. A smaller microbe, like a virus, could have gotten through the filtering.

Earlier, these and other scientists had feared that a virus might be responsible for damaging the immune systems in gay men and drug users and paving the way for the cases of *Pneumocystis*. Now the same combination—a weakened immune system and the rare pneumonia—had turned up in a hemophiliac. This seemed to be added proof that the guilty party was a virus. A virus that could be transmitted in blood products like Factor VIII.

The scientists reasoned that the virus had come from one of the many people who had donated blood for the clotting substance. But how had it gotten into that person's blood? Was the donor a gay man who had acquired the virus in the course of sex? Or a drug user who had been infected through an injection? One question led to another and then another. . . .

The scientists knew there was only one way to find answers to these questions—thorough, in-depth research studies. And a number of important projects were launched. The effects of Kaposi's sarcoma in gay men were analyzed in a special clinic at San Francisco's

General Hospital. A New York doctor conducted tests on five children of female drug users, hoping to discover why all the children had impaired immune systems and several were suffering from *Pneumocystis*. The national Centers for Disease Control organized a task force to investigate the outbreaks of Kaposi's sarcoma and *Pneumocystis* in San Francisco, New York, Los Angeles, and other U.S. cities. Detailed personal histories, including lists of sexual partners, were taken on all patients with the two diseases.

But the scientists faced a crippling obstacle as they attempted to pursue these and other studies. Only limited funds were available for research. And given the political mood of the country, those funds were more likely to be cut back than increased.

CHAPTER TWELVE

FRUSTRATIONS AND FEARS

Ronald Reagan had been elected President in November 1980, on a platform that emphasized two chief goals: to cut all Federal spending except for defense, and to lower taxes. Now, in 1981 and 1982, officials at the Centers for Disease Control, the National Institutes of Health, and other government agencies concerned with public health were finding it difficult to maintain their current programs, let alone obtain additional funds for research on a mystery virus.

Besides the lack of money, scientists in the health field had to contend with numerous other obstacles. One of the most serious was a lack of public sympathy for those hit hardest by the disease: gay men and intravenous drug users. Knowing this, the mass media continued to pay scant attention to the epidemic.

Gay writers like playwright Larry Kramer were

outraged. In a letter to a New York gay newspaper, Kramer wrote: "If Kaposi's sarcoma were a new form of cancer attacking straight people, it would be receiving constant media attention, and pressure from every side would be so great upon the cancer-funding institutions that research would be proceeding with great intensity."

Gays themselves put roadblocks in the way of some scientific investigations. When researchers suggested that the promiscuous sex practiced in bathhouses might be helping to spread the disease, gays reacted angrily. They had fought too long and too hard for their sexual freedom to give it up now, they said. Besides, nothing had been proved about how the disease was caused, had it?

Larry Kramer challenged this position. ". . . Something we are doing is ticking off the time bomb that is causing the breakdown of immunity in certain bodies, and while it is true that we don't know what it is specifically, isn't it better to be cautious until various suspected causes have been discounted rather than reckless . . . ?"

Few gays were yet ready to heed Kramer's advice. Some even accused him of being a traitor to his fellows. Meanwhile, the condition acquired a new name: Gay-Related Immune Deficiency, or GRID. The label was misleading, since by then the disease had claimed many nongay victims.

FRESH EVIDENCE

Despite the obstacles, and the inaccurate name, U.S. scientists made some important advances in their understanding of GRID during 1982. Fresh evidence that it was a blood-borne virus transmitted through sex came when researchers on both coasts compared notes on the doings of Gaetan Dugas, an unusually handsome flight attendant from French Canada.

Dugas had been treated for Kaposi's sarcoma the year before at the New York University Medical Center. While there, he had boasted to an interviewer about his sexual contacts in cities all across the U.S. and Canada. Now medical researchers in Los Angeles discovered that four of the first nineteen patients with GRID in that city had had sex with Gaetan Dugas. And four others had gone to bed with men who had been involved with the flight attendant.

Besides tracing a clear pattern of infection for the first time, this discovery verified something that many scientists had already begun to suspect. The disease had a long incubation period between the time of infection with the virus and the appearance of the first symptoms. One of the Los Angeles GRID victims showed no symptoms until ten months after the weekend he had spent with Gaetan Dugas. Another Los Angeles man noticed his first Kaposi's sarcoma lesions thirteen months after his encounter with the flight attendant.

By July 1982, new cases of GRID were being reported to the Centers for Disease Control at the rate of two and a half a day, and there were now cases in twenty-four of the fifty states. The CDC began to call this outbreak of immune deficiency an epidemic.

Another hemophiliac who had been taking Factor VIII to help clot his blood died of *Pnemocystis* that summer at a hospital in Denver, Colorado. Yet another case involving a hemophiliac surfaced in Canton, Ohio. Realizing the nation's blood supply was endangered, the CDC recommended that guidelines for donors be established. People at risk for GRID, such as gay men and drug users, would be asked to stop donating or selling their blood.

The National Hemophilia Foundation immediately attacked the suggested guidelines, saying there wasn't enough evidence of a connection between Factor VIII and the cases of GRID to justify them. The Foundation feared it would lose valuable sources of blood if the guidelines were put in place. It was also reluctant to admit there could be anything wrong with the supplies of Factor VIII, which had been of such benefit to hemophiliacs.

Gay organizations joined in opposing the CDC guidelines. Any move to screen and reject blood donors would have serious civil rights implications for millions of Americans, gay leaders said.

The Food and Drug Administration, which was responsible for regulating the blood industry, took note of the controversy and decided to adopt a wait-and-see attitude. In the meantime, all parties concerned agreed that a more neutral and accurate name for the disease was needed.

THE FINAL NAME

Someone from the CDC suggested Acquired Immune Deficiency Syndrome, and Dr. Bruce Voeller, a scientist and gay activist, said it could be called AIDS for short. The word "acquired" indicated that the disease came from somewhere outside the person and was not inborn. "Syndrome" referred to the large variety of symptoms that characterized the disease, and the name as a whole had no sexual connotations.

On August 2, 1982, television commentator Dan Rather mentioned AIDS for the first time on the *CBS Nightly News*. "Federal health officials consider it an epidemic," Rather said. "Yet you rarely hear a thing about it."

That may have been true of the media. But despite a continuing lack of funds, scientists were hard at work behind the scenes, piecing together bits and pieces of information about the disease that they had gathered. Then came a new development that confirmed one of the scientists' worst fears.

The year before, a baby born in San Francisco to a healthy young couple had required a series of blood transfusions. Seven months later, the baby came down with a yeast infection in his mouth and other symptoms of AIDS. Now, in the fall of 1982, researchers learned that one of the thirteen donors whose blood had been transfused into the baby had since died of AIDS himself.

Although there had been some suspicious cases earlier, this was the first documented instance in the U.S. of AIDS contracted through a blood transfusion. It raised new and alarming questions about the safety of the nation's blood supply.

In response, the Centers for Disease Control proposed that all blood used for transfusions and in the manufacture of Factor VIII be tested for antibodies to hepatitis B. Virtually all those at risk for AIDS, from gay men to intravenous drug users, had had that form of hepatitis at some time in their lives. The hepatitis virus disappeared after recovery, but antibodies to it remained in the patient's bloodstream.

Blood bankers objected to the CDC proposal. Dr. Joseph Bove, director of the blood bank at Yale University, was quoted as saying, "We are contemplating all these wide-ranging measures because one baby got AIDS after transfusion from a person who later came down with AIDS and there may be a few other cases."

A spokesman for the CDC retorted, "To bury our heads in the sand and say, 'Let's wait for more cases' is not an adequate public health policy."

The discussions concluded with the blood bankers declaring it would cost too much—an estimated $800 million or more annually—to test their blood supplies for hepatitis B antibodies. They would continue to pursue a wait-and-see policy instead.

The CDC representatives could hardly believe it. They felt the blood bankers were making a terrible mistake, one that would result in the loss of many additional lives. And, in the light of later events, they were right. But there was nothing the CDC could do in the early months of 1983 to make the blood industry test its products.

Nor could the CDC or any other government agency close gay bathhouses and sex clubs, although evidence was mounting that they were prime locations for the transmission of AIDS. Interviews with gay men suffering from the disease in San Francisco, New York, and Los Angeles revealed that many of them had patronized bathhouses, where they had engaged in anal intercourse without the protection of a condom.

Scientists had long suspected that the virus was transmitted via semen and other bodily fluids. If they were correct, it would be easy for the virus to get into a person's bloodstream through a cut or abrasion during unprotected anal intercourse. At a meeting in San Francisco with leaders of gay organizations, Dr. Robert Bolan of the Bay Area Physicians for Human Rights warned: "You have to avoid contact with bodily fluids. That would include semen, urine, and blood. This is the big enchilada, guys. You don't get a second chance once you get this."

One of the gay leaders, Bill Kraus, agreed with the doctor. "We believe it is time to speak the simple truth— and to care enough about one another to act on it. Unsafe sex is—quite literally—killing us. . . . Unsafe sex at bathhouses and sex clubs is particularly dangerous." This was one of the first times anyone had used the expression *unsafe sex*. Soon it and its opposite, *safe sex*, would figure in almost every discussion of AIDS. And some time after that, the phrase *safer sex* began to be used, to reflect the fact that condoms are not infallible.

Unfortunately, most of the other gay leaders present at the meeting disagreed with Kraus. Like the representatives of the blood banks and the manufacturers of Factor VIII, they questioned whether the CDC and the doctors *really* knew how AIDS was transmitted. Until there was more solid evidence, the leaders saw no reason why the bathhouses and clubs should be monitored, let alone closed.

As more reports came in of people getting AIDS from blood transfusions, the media began to pay more attention to the disease. *Newsweek* magazine ran a cover story with a banner headline that read: "EPIDEMIC: The Mysterious and Deadly Disease Called AIDS May Be the Public-Health Threat of the Century. How Did It Start? Can It Be Stopped?" Other magazines and newspapers followed suit with stories of their own, and TV newscasters gave the epidemic more coverage also.

IRRATIONAL FEARS

Because so little was known about AIDS, the stories stirred up fears in many of those who read and viewed them. If the nation's blood supply was tainted, what else was dangerous? Could the disease be transmitted by routine household contacts like drinking from the same glass or sitting on the same toilet seat?

Scientists from the CDC and elsewhere tried to reassure the public that routine contacts were safe, but not everyone believed them. Some jurors on a case in San Francisco passed a note to the judge that read, "We the undersigned protest having to sit in a confined space with an admitted victim of a fatal disease which has baffled science. . . ." The juror in question, the "admitted victim," resigned from the jury rather than have his illness get in the way of its deliberations.

Inmates at a prison in Auburn, New York, went on a hunger strike because the cafeteria was still putting out eating utensils that a prisoner who had died of AIDS had used. A number of funeral directors in New York City were reluctant to embalm AIDS victims, fearing the bodies might be contaminated.

Medical workers felt particularly vulnerable and took special precautions to defend themselves against infection. Doctors, dentists, nurses, and paramedics all began to wear face masks, rubber gloves, and sometimes protective suits when working with suspected AIDS patients. Gradually, health professionals began to wear protective gear no matter whom they were treating.

Like those physicians who deserted their patients in the face of the Black Death, some physicians in the 1980s flatly refused to treat people with AIDS. They tried to justify their denial of treatment on the ground that it presented an unacceptable hazard to them personally.

Both the American Medical Association and the American College of Physicians rejected this argument, stating: "Refusal of a physician to care for a specific category of patients—for example, patients who have AIDS—is morally and ethically indefensible."

The issues of morals and morality came up in other quarters as media coverage of the AIDS epidemic increased. The conservative columnist Patrick J. Buchanan wrote, "The poor homosexuals—they have declared war on nature, and now nature is exacting an awful retribution."

Some clergymen saw the epidemic as an expression of God's wrath. In a statement that sounded remarkably similar to some made by clergymen at the time of the Black Death and during early smallpox epidemics, the Rev. Jerry Falwell said: "When you violate moral, health, and hygiene laws, you reap the whirlwind. You cannot shake your fist in God's face and get away with it."

A gang of teenagers in Seattle decided to stand in for God and exact their own vengeance. Wielding baseball bats, the youths rampaged through a public park frequented by gays. They shouted "diseased queers" and "plague-carrying faggots" as they beat up every man unlucky enough to cross their path. After his arrest, one of the attackers tried to defend his actions. "If we don't kill these fags, they'll kill us with their f...... AIDS disease," he said.

Fortunately, most people did not react to the epidemic and its casualties in such a negative fashion. In fact, there were encouraging developments on both the political and scientific fronts in the spring and summer of 1983. Although the Reagan administration did not request them, the U.S. Congress voted $12 million in new federal funds for AIDS research. At almost the same time, Dr. Robert Gallo, one of the nation's most prominent scientists in the field of viral diseases, announced that he was going to concentrate on finding the cause of AIDS.

Dr. Gallo would pursue his research at the National Cancer Institute in Bethesda, Maryland. "I believe a retrovirus is involved," he said, "and we're going to prove or disprove it within a year."

Retroviruses make up a unique subgroup of viruses that are found in both humans and animals. Like other viruses, they infect by attaching themselves to and penetrating susceptible cells in the body. But then, unlike ordinary viruses, the retrovirus tricks the host cell into reproducing it as though it were part of the cell's own genetic material. Dr. Gallo had made his reputation as a scientist when he discovered a new retrovirus, HTLV, that caused one kind of leukemia in humans. Now he was convinced that another retrovirus, maybe a variation of HTLV, caused AIDS.

Gallo was a competitive man who always wanted to be the first to make a research discovery. Spurring him on now were reports from France that scientists at the Pasteur Institute in Paris had also been searching for an AIDS virus. Some of the reports said the French were close to finding it, if they had not already done so.

CHAPTER THIRTEEN

ONE MYSTERY IS SOLVED

French doctors and scientists had been aware that a new disease was loose in the world ever since three of its victims showed up at Paris hospitals in the late 1970s. All three were from central Africa, or had spent time there, and they were all suffering from PCP.

Unlike their American counterparts, the French medical experts did not link the disease to gay males, since one of the first victims was a heterosexual man and the other two were women. But they did decide early on that it must be caused by a virus.

Since swollen lymph glands are one of the earliest symptoms of the disease, the French thought the best place to start the search for a virus would be in the lymph nodes of an AIDS patient. In January 1983, they removed a small piece of a patient's node and put it into a culture of T cells at the Pasteur Institute in Paris. The French knew of the HTLV virus that Robert Gallo had discovered. If the mystery virus in the lymph node resembled HTLV—and the French thought it probably did—then they should soon see a growth of T cells as the virus infected the culture.

The French monitored the culture every three days, and added more T cells when the original batch seemed to be dying off. A radioactive test of the culture on the eighteenth day showed that a retrovirus was indeed growing at a rapid rate within it. But the virus did not behave like HTLV. Instead of generating a vast number of new white T cells, this virus was so lethal that it killed off the existing cells.

The French scientists were sure they had discovered a new retrovirus, but they knew they would have to gather conclusive evidence to prove its existence. First, they gave it a name: LAV, which stood for lymph-associated virus since it had been taken originally from an infected lymph node. Later, they also succeeded in detecting LAV in the blood of several hemophiliacs who displayed symptoms of AIDS. But Luc Montagnier, the Pasteur Institute scientist who was directing the research, still hadn't figured out to which family of viruses LAV belonged. If it wasn't a variant of HTLV, what was it?

Like so many scientific discoveries, the answer

came by accident. During a meeting with Montagnier, another researcher at the Institute happened to mention a family of viruses found mainly in animals. The viruses were called *lentiviruses*, *lenti* meaning slow. They acquired this name because they lay dormant for quite a while after getting into the animal's cells. Then they became extremely active.

His curiosity aroused, Montagnier proceeded to investigate lentiviruses. The more he learned about them, the more he became convinced that LAV was a lentivirus also. It contained the same proteins. It resembled a lentivirus in photographs take with the aid of an electron microscope. And, like a lentivirus, it could remain dormant for months or even years in human cells before developing into AIDS.

The French presented their research findings about LAV at several international conferences, and a number of American scientists from the Centers for Disease Control were impressed by them. The Americans asked for samples of LAV that they could study at their laboratories in Atlanta.

Robert Gallo was unconvinced. He suggested to colleagues that LAV was not a human virus at all, and continued to believe that a form of HTLV caused AIDS. But as he and his staff pursued their research on HTLV without success, Gallo began to worry that the

French might be proved right and he would not get the credit for discovering the AIDS virus.

In September 1983, the Pasteur Institute sent samples of their LAV virus to Gallo. The French hoped the samples would help to prove their case that LAV was not related to HTLV but was a different virus altogether.

By January 1984, Gallo had succeeded in growing twenty different cultures of the AIDS virus on his own. He still maintained, however, that it was not a new virus but a variant of HTLV. Consequently, he called it HTLV-III.

At almost the same time, the French offered the most convincing proof yet that their virus, LAV, caused AIDS. The U.S. Centers for Disease Control had shipped thirty blood samples to the scientists at the Pasteur Institute. Ten of the samples were from gay men who had developed AIDS, ten came from gay men who had swollen lymph glands but no other symptoms as yet, and the remaining ten samples were from heterosexuals who were not at risk for AIDS. Although the samples were not identified for them, to avoid biased results, the French scientists found antibodies to the LAV virus in all twenty of the blood samples from gay men. They found none in the ten blood samples taken from uninfected heterosexuals.

Further studies revealed that the French LAV and

Dr. Gallo's HTLV-III were one and the same virus. Excitement ran high in the French and American laboratories where the scientific research had been carried out. For the moment, the question of who discovered what was forgotten. All that mattered was that the virus that caused AIDS had been found. The mystery was solved.

Margaret Heckler, Secretary of Health and Human Services in the Reagan administration, called a press conference on April 23, 1984, to announce the discovery of HTLV-III. "Today we add another miracle to the long honor roll of American medicine and science," Secretary Heckler said. She mentioned the contributions of the French scientists, but saved most of her praise for Dr. Gallo and his colleagues at the National Cancer Institute.

The overall mood of the press conference was optimistic. But some scientists present couldn't help but wonder what they might have accomplished if more funds for research had been available when the first cases of AIDS came to light back in 1981. They might have succeeded in finding the virus as early as 1982, before the disease had made such inroads in the population. By the day of the conference, 4,177 cases of AIDS had been reported in the United States and 1,807 of them had already died.

THE PATH OF THE VIRUS

Once the AIDS virus had been discovered, the path the disease had taken around the world could be traced more accurately.

Blood tests in the African nation of Zaire revealed that as much as twelve percent of the rural population was infected with the virus. This and other statistics led researchers to conclude that AIDS had originated somewhere in central Africa. It also explained why Dr. Grethe Rask had been one of the first Western victims of the disease. She had worked at hospitals in Zaire, where she no doubt had come into contact with the blood of infected patients.

The human AIDS virus is remarkably similar in composition to a virus found in African monkeys. Scientists speculated that at some point the virus made the leap to humans, perhaps when the members of a remote tribe killed some infected monkeys and were exposed to their blood. As more and more Africans moved from the countryside into cities, the disease probably came with them, mutating to its present lethal form. The crowded conditions in poor urban neighborhoods would have enabled it to spread more rapidly.

From Africa, the disease was carried to Europe by people like Dr. Grethe Rask. Haitians who worked in

Zaire in the 1970s probably brought the virus along when they returned to their native island. Gay men from New York and other American cities frequently vacationed in Haiti. They could have contracted the disease there and unwittingly spread it when they got back home.

Now, with the virus in hand, the National Institutes of Health drew up plans to test the nation's blood supply. The Food and Drug Administration still didn't think such testing was essential, and gay organizations feared the test results might be misused, but the National Cancer Institute made the test its number-one AIDS priority. It took over a Maryland research facility and got ready to produce the 750 gallons of virus that would be needed each month to test all the blood used in transfusions. Congress appropriated $8 million to help cover the initial costs.

In March 1985, the federal government gave its approval to the first AIDS antibody test. Supplies of the test were distributed immediately to more than 2,300 blood banks and plasma centers all across the United States.

The test works much like the antibody tests already in use for hepatitis and other diseases. A small plastic bead is coated with the AIDS virus and placed in a little well. When a drop of blood is added to the well, any antibodies to the AIDS virus that are in the blood latch onto the coating of virus around the bead. To detect them, the bead is washed with various dyes and chemicals. If antibodies have gotten into the coating, the bead will turn purple.

Most of the blood tested by this method was found to be free of antibodies that indicated the presence of the AIDS virus. But those few batches that were tainted could now be spotted and discarded before they did any harm. From 1985 on, the chances of contracting the AIDS virus from a blood transfusion or a faulty batch of the Factor VIII compound used by hemophiliacs were almost entirely eliminated.

The federal government did not ignore the concerns of gays as the AIDS antibody test began to be applied throughout the United States. Under an agreement reached between the Food and Drug Administration and several prominent gay organizations, each test kit was labeled with a warning: "It is inappropriate to use this test as a screen for AIDS or as a screen for members of groups at increased risk for AIDS in the general population," the warning read.

TO TEST OR NOT TO TEST?

This measure reassured gays that test results would be kept confidential and not become an excuse for discrimination. But it did nothing to dispel an even more worrisome question gays had about the antibody test.

Now that it was readily available, should they have themselves tested to find out whether they were infected with the AIDS virus?

For many gay men, this was one of the most difficult personal decisions they would ever have to make. If the results were negative, they would feel immense relief. But if they tested positive, they would have to live with the knowledge that at any time they might fall victim to a deadly disease like *Pneumocystis* or Kaposi's sarcoma.

On the other hand, a decision not to be tested created another kind of psychological burden. What if they were carrying a lethal virus with which they could infect others, perhaps those closest to them? Wouldn't it be better to know their status so that they could adjust their behavior accordingly?

Scientists and health officials advocated testing as many of those at risk for AIDS as possible. In this way, they could get a more accurate idea of the number of people who were infected, and estimate what would be needed in the way of medical, social, and financial resources to combat the disease. At the same time, the scientists and doctors recognized that, in a democracy, there was no way they could compel anyone to be tested. Only the U.S. armed forces had the authority—which they invoked—to screen all new recruits for the AIDS virus and reject those who tested positive.

While these issues were being debated, Dr. Robert Gallo and his colleagues at the National Cancer Institute had made some alarming new discoveries about the nature of the AIDS virus. After evaluating the statistics, Gallo raised his estimate of the number of people infected with the virus who would develop one of the serious illnesses associated with AIDS (a stage of the infection that came to be called "full-blown AIDS") from one in twenty-five to one in seven.

Gallo also learned that, besides infecting and destroying white T cells, the virus is able to get through the barrier that normally keeps microbes away from the brain and attack vital brain cells. Now he understood why AIDS patients often suffered severe depression and memory loss, and sometimes sank into madness.

Gallo discovered that the AIDS virus could assume somewhat different forms in different people. This raised a new fear: Would scientists be able to develop an effective vaccine against AIDS, since what worked against one form of the virus might not work against another?

Other scientists had more hopeful news to report. Tests on the family members of AIDS-affected hemophiliacs revealed that none of them had become infected with the virus. Similar results occurred when hundreds of doctors, nurses, and medical technicians who worked closely with AIDS patients had themselves tested. With this evidence in hand, the scientists determined once and for all that AIDS could not be contracted through casual contact. It took a heavy dose of the virus, fed directly into the bloodstream, to transmit the disease.

New information on the mechanics of transmission was coming in almost daily. Researchers in New York, Chicago, and other cities confirmed that the virus circulated among intravenous drug users when they shared needles ("works") with an infected person. The virus could also be passed from an infected mother to her child during pregnancy, at birth, or through her breast milk. The majority of these mothers were drug users themselves, or the wives and sex partners of users.

Medical workers in San Francisco found the virus in the vaginal fluids of a female prostitute who came to a hospital emergency room for treatment. This helped to explain how AIDS could be transmitted from women to men—a common form of transmission in many African and southeast Asian countries, but still relatively uncommon in the United States.

Other medical workers located the virus in the semen of both a gay man suffering from full-blown AIDS and another gay man who showed no symptoms as yet. Their discovery proved two things: that the virus could be transmitted in a man's semen during anal or oral sex—something many gay spokesmen had tried to deny up to this point—and that it could be spread by men who appeared to be healthy.

In light of this new evidence, San Francisco moved at last to close its bathhouses and sex clubs. "Today [October 9, 1984] I have ordered the closure of fourteen commercial establishments that promote and profit from the spread of AIDS," said Dr. Mervyn Silverman, director of the city's Department of Public Health. "These businesses have been inspected on a number of occasions and demonstrate a blatant disregard for the health of their patrons and the community. . . . Make no mistake about it: These fourteen establishments are not fostering gay liberation. They are fostering disease and death."

Although they did not follow suit immediately, other cities such as New York and Los Angeles eventually closed their bathhouses also. There were surprisingly few protests from gay organizations. By this stage of the epidemic, most people—even some of the more militant gay liberationists—agreed the baths and sex clubs were a health hazard.

SEARCHING FOR DRUGS

Scientists in the United States and France now focused their efforts on the search for drugs that would slow down or stop the replication of the AIDS virus in the cells it invaded. One doctor at the Centers for Disease Control proposed testing ribavirin, a drug that had shown some success against flu viruses. At the Pasteur Institute in Paris, scientists were testing an antiviral drug called HPA-23, which had halted the replication of a leukemia retrovirus in laboratory mice.

The scientists had to overcome many hurdles as they pursued their research. Viruses and retroviruses are not independent life forms like bacterial organisms. Instead, they are pieces of genetic material that become part of the cells they infect. To kill the virus, you have to kill the cell also, and risk damaging side effects. Consequently, science has yet to develop any completely effective treatments for viral diseases such as the flu or the common cold. Vaccines can create antibodies that protect people against infection in the first place, but they cannot provide cures for those who are already infected.

Another hurdle was a continuing lack of funds for research. Although Health Secretary Margaret Heckler kept saying that her department considered AIDS its "number-one priority," she requested no additional appropriations from Congress. And, probably out of deference to his conservative supporters, President Ronald Reagan had never spoken the word AIDS in any public utterance. Nor had he given any other indication that he knew an epidemic was going on.

Faced with this lack of interest, gay men and other concerned individuals banded together to help those afflicted with AIDS. In New York City, Gay Men's Health Crisis (GMHC), which Larry Kramer had helped found in 1982 to raise money for AIDS research, ventured into many other areas of activity. By late 1984, it operated an AIDS hotline to provide up-to-date information about the disease. It also offered free legal advice to people who had tested positive for the virus or were suffering from full-blown AIDS, and had established a buddy system of volunteers who helped AIDS patients with shopping, trips to the doctor, and household management.

Similar organizations sprang up in San Francisco, San Antonio, and other U.S. cities. In San Francisco, the Shanti Project started with rap sessions for gay men suffering from Kaposi's sarcoma. From there it went on to offer grief counseling to people with AIDS and those close to them, and to create residences where homeless AIDS patients could receive both shelter and care.

Frustrated by the lack of effective drugs or a vaccine, some AIDS patients turned in desperation to various forms of alternative medicine. These included the practice of vegetarianism, Chinese herbal medicine, art and music therapy, yoga exercises, and diets that made wide use of garlic, shiitake mushrooms, and blue-green algae. Such treatments might offer hope to the patient and make him forget his troubles for a time. But there was no solid evidence that any of them slowed or halted the progress of the disease any more than the "red treatment" was effective against smallpox.

Those patients who could afford it sometimes traveled to Paris, France, after hearing that experimental treatments there with the drug HPA-23 had brought promising results. One of those who made the trip, quietly and without publicity, in September 1984, was a famous movie actor who had been diagnosed with Kaposi's sarcoma earlier in the year.

The actor was given large doses of HPA-23 for several weeks, and at the conclusion of the treatment was told that his blood showed no trace of the AIDS virus. He returned to Hollywood thinking he was cured. But within a few months the actor experienced extreme fatigue, and then he began to lose weight again. . . .

CHAPTER FOURTEEN

AN ACTOR NAMED ROCK

From the time he came to Hollywood in the late 1940s, Rock Hudson always played ruggedly masculine roles. But in his carefully concealed private life he was exclusively gay.

A muscular six-footer, Hudson—whose real name was Roy Fitzgerald—had served in the U.S. Navy before heading west to try his luck in the movies. His agent renamed him Rock Hudson because he thought it sounded more macho.

After acting in a string of routine westerns and action dramas, Hudson got a chance to play the romantic lead in *The Magnificent Obsession* opposite Jane Wyman, Ronald Reagan's ex-wife. The picture was a huge success and made Hudson one of the most popular male stars of the 1950s and 1960s. In *Pillow Talk* he romanced Doris Day, in the epic *Giant* he married Elizabeth

Taylor. Meanwhile, in the privacy of his home and on frequent trips to San Francisco, he lived the life of an active homosexual.

By the early 1980s, Hudson was still making an occasional movie but was seen more frequently as a guest star in television series like *Dynasty*. It was at this time that he first noticed the small purple spot on his neck—a lesion that his doctors diagnosed as Kaposi's sarcoma.

After being treated with the experimental drug in Paris, Hudson returned to the U.S. and resumed his career. But by the summer of 1985 it was clear that the treatments hadn't worked. He felt extremely weak and kept on losing weight.

Hudson told friends he planned to return to Paris for further treatment as soon as he was strong enough. First, though, he wanted to fulfill a promise he'd made to his former co-star and friend, Doris Day, to help her launch her new television show on the Christian Broadcasting Network.

When Hudson showed up for a press conference with Day before the start of filming, reporters were shocked by how old and haggard the star looked. Some of his responses to their questions were vague and rambling, and they noticed that he seemed to have trouble walking. Hudson's publicity representative assured the reporters that the actor was simply recovering from a bad case of flu, and he managed to get through the two days of taping. It would be his last appearance on film.

The job done, Hudson left almost immediately for Paris. But he collapsed in the lobby of his hotel there before he could resume treatments with the experimental AIDS drug at the Pasteur Institute. He was rushed to a hospital, where it was first announced that he was suffering from liver cancer and then that it was merely a case of "fatigue and general malaise." Hudson's old Hollywood friend Ronald Reagan phoned from the White House to wish him well and let the actor know that he and Nancy Reagan were keeping him in their thoughts and prayers.

Stories began to spread in France and the United States that Hudson really had AIDS. Now the star and those around him were faced with a crucial decision. Should they go on trying to hide his actual condition, or should they reveal the truth? They decided in favor of the truth. On July 25, 1985, a French publicist issued this brief statement to the press: "Mr. Hudson has Acquired Immune Deficiency Syndrome."

Those seven words had significant implications. Not just for Rock Hudson, but for the course of the epidemic and all those who were caught up in it. Till then AIDS was considered such a stigma that few of its victims, famous or unknown, had admitted they had the disease. Even in obituaries the cause of death was concealed. Now a popular movie star had gone public with his illness. "What has happened for America is that someone they know is being affected," said Dr. James Curran, head of the AIDS task force at the Centers for Disease Control.

Since Hudson was too far gone to be treated again at the Pasteur Institute, he flew home to Los Angeles on a chartered jet. TV news cameras positioned on rooftops at the airport awaited the plane's arrival. They got only a few brief, distant shots as the actor was lifted down from the jet and carried to a waiting helicopter for the short flight to the UCLA Medical Center.

That was the last time Rock Hudson was ever seen in public. But on September 19, a statement from him was read in Los Angeles at a gala benefit dinner to raise funds for AIDS research. "I am not happy that I am sick," the actor said. "I am not happy that I have AIDS, but if that is helping others, I can, at least, know that my own misfortune has had some positive worth." The affair raised more than $1 million, $250,000 of which was contributed by the actor.

Rock Hudson died of complications from AIDS in October 1985. Along with his movies, the actor left another valuable legacy. Thanks to him, a new degree of openness and honesty had been introduced into the media's coverage of AIDS. And public awareness of the disease and its consequences had been broadened considerably.

Carrying the discussion further was an unlikely government spokesman, Dr. C. Everett Koop. President Reagan had appointed Koop, a well-known conservative and leader in the antiabortion movement, to be Surgeon General of the United States in 1981. Now, in 1986, it seemed a safe bet that Koop would adopt a hard-line conservative position when the President asked him to write a comprehensive report on the AIDS epidemic. Instead, he surprised everyone.

Koop spent much of the year interviewing scientists, health officials, and even the leaders of gay organizations. When the report was finished, he ordered 10,000 copies to be printed without letting the White House see the manuscript in advance. The report turned out to be a far-reaching call to arms against the epidemic. It avoided both politics and moralizing, and emphasized the need for a strenuous campaign to inform the public about the disease.

Koop urged that AIDS education "start at the earliest grade possible." Drug users should be alerted to the dangers of sharing needles and syringes. Gay men, heterosexual drug users, and others with multiple sex partners were advised to adopt safer sex practices. Going against the policies of many religious groups, the report advocated the widespread use of condoms to aid in halting the spread of the disease.

Right-wing conservatives reacted with predictable

outrage to the Surgeon General's report. The antifeminist leader Phyllis Schlafly said Koop's sex-education recommendations could lead to grade-school classes in sodomy. But those who had lobbied for a more rational, humane approach to the epidemic hailed the report's conclusions. They noted that, by 1987, the United States—which had the largest number of reported AIDS cases of any industrialized nation—was the only one that had not launched a major education campaign against the disease.

THE PRESIDENT SPEAKS AT LAST

The call for more in the way of AIDS education reached even into the White House. In May 1987, after carefully maintaining his silence on the subject for six years, President Ronald Reagan finally agreed to give a talk about the epidemic at a Washington fund-raiser for the American Foundation for AIDS Research (AmFAR), the organization Rock Hudson had helped launch. Meanwhile, the virus that caused AIDS had acquired a new name, agreed on in negotiations between the French and American scientists who had discovered it. The virus was now known as the Human Immuno-deficiency Virus, or HIV.

In his speech at the fund-raiser, President Reagan emphasized the need for more AIDS antibody tests but said nothing about civil rights protection or confidentiality guarantees for those who tested positive. Nor did he mention gays. He spoke only of what are sometimes called the disease's "innocent victims"—hemophiliacs, transfusion recipients, and the spouses and children of intravenous drug addicts. The president obviously could not bring himself to acknowledge the many homosexual men who had suffered and died because of AIDS, even though one of them was his good friend Rock Hudson.

By the time President Reagan spoke about AIDS on that May night in 1987, 36,058 Americans had been diagnosed with the disease and 20,849 had died.

The fund-raiser took place during the Third International Conference on AIDS, which was held that year in Washington. The best news to come out of the conference centered on an antiviral drug called AZT. Trials starting the previous year had shown that the drug successfully interfered with the replication of HIV in T cells. It could have toxic side effects—prolonged nausea, vomiting, fatigue—but it was the first drug that extended the lives of AIDS patients. In 1985, before treatment with AZT began, only about 31% of patients lived longer than two years after being diagnosed with full-blown AIDS. By 1987, the percentage had increased to 49%.

Unfortunately, there were no other major breakthroughs in treatment in the next few years. Several other antiviral drugs were approved for use, but none of them completely halted the spread of HIV. And fresh evidence that the virus could assume many different forms dashed hopes for the early development of a vaccine to prevent infection in the first place.

Impatient with the slow pace of AIDS research, Larry Kramer and others founded a militant new organization known as ACT UP (AIDS Coalition To Unleash Power), most of whose members were gay. The group staged noisy demonstrations in New York and other cities to press for the faster release of promising new drugs, and to get manufacturers to lower prices on existing drugs like AZT.

ACT UP members also protested what they saw as the indifference of government bureaucracies and organized religion to those suffering from AIDS. In one widely publicized "zap," they went so far as to disrupt a mass at New York City's St. Patrick's Cathedral. ACT UP probably made more enemies than friends as a result of such demonstrations, but the organization did help to focus public attention on AIDS and speed the development of several new drugs.

In the meantime, many of the disease's victims were still being ostracized by their peers despite all the evidence that showed AIDS could not be contracted through casual contact. One of these sufferers was an Indiana teenager, a hemophiliac named Ryan White.

CHAPTER FIFTEEN

"A NORMAL HAPPY TEENAGER"

Ryan White always knew that he had hemophilia. Born on December 6, 1971, he was circumcised when he was just three days old and failed to stop bleeding. His doctors realized immediately that he was a hemophiliac. They gave him massive transfusions to replace the blood he had lost and managed to save the infant's life.

As he grew older, Ryan often got bad bruises when he played, but regular injections of Factor VIII helped to keep his hemophilia under control. This was in the days when no one had ever heard of a disease called AIDS, or seen any need to test the blood from which Factor VIII came for antibodies to the virus.

By 1984, Ryan was an average kid of twelve who collected comic books, loved cars, and liked to eat pizza. He still relied on injections of Factor VIII, which

his divorced mother, Jeanne, had learned how to admin-
ister to him. What neither of them guessed was that the
lifesaving blood product had become a potential killer.
For it was Factor VIII that gave Ryan AIDS.

Soon after school started in September 1984, he
experienced the first symptoms: stomach cramps and
diarrhea, followed by night sweats that soaked his
sheets. It was hard for him to enjoy his thirteenth
birthday in December because he'd developed a cough
he couldn't shake. Almost unable to breathe, he was
rushed from his hometown of Kokomo to a special
children's hospital in Indianapolis. Doctors there operated on Ryan and discovered that he was suffering from
Pneumocystis—the rare type of pneumonia associated
with AIDS.

Ryan's mother didn't tell him he had the disease until after Christmas, and it was February before he could
go home. But he was determined, with the support of
his mother and sister, not to let AIDS get the best of
him and to live as normal a life as he could. That became more and more difficult as the spring wore on.

His mother sued the manufacturers of Factor VIII,
charging they were to blame for Ryan's illness and
should help to pay his medical expenses. Word of the
lawsuit got out, and the local paper ran a story revealing
that Ryan had AIDS. After that, some of their neighbors
began to avoid Ryan and his family. When they went to

church, they were asked to sit by themselves in either the first or last row. But the worst was yet to come.

In July, officials at Western High School let Ryan know they didn't want him to return in the fall. They were afraid he would infect the other students. His mother wasn't sure what to do, but Ryan wanted to fight back. "If we don't, we won't be allowed to go anywhere or do anything," he said.

The health commissioner of Indiana called Western and told the principal that if Ryan wasn't sick, he belonged in school. But the school board voted to keep him out. Fifty teachers at the high school said they would refuse to teach him. And parents circulated a petition supporting the school board's action, saying, "We must protect our children." It was an expression of the community's fear—the same sort of fear that led people in Italy and France to wall up victims of the Black Death in their homes.

Ryan's lawyer filed a lawsuit to get the school to readmit him, and the Concerned Citizens and Parents group threatened to countersue if the school backed down. The principal of Western tried to satisfy everyone by arranging a two-way phone hookup so that Ryan could take part in his classes while remaining at home.

Reluctantly Ryan agreed to the plan; he really wanted to be back at school with his friends. There were problems with the hookup, also. When his teachers moved around the classroom, he couldn't hear them, and he often had trouble hearing his classmates, too.

Meanwhile, the local and national media had picked up on the story. Television news programs broadcast lengthy accounts of Ryan's struggle to return to school. He became an instant celebrity, receiving thousands of letters of support from all over the country.

The stories only seemed to harden the attitudes of people in Kokomo. One boy Ryan barely knew phoned to ask why he spit and sneezed on vegetables at the supermarket. At a skating rink another kid asked if it was true he spit on people when he was mad. Some parents forbade their children to see Ryan. Obviously, these people still believed AIDS could be spread through casual contact.

At a hearing three doctors testified that Ryan would be no threat to anyone if he went back to school. Shortly thereafter the hearing officer announced her decision: Western High School could not legally bar Ryan from attending classes in person.

Preparations were made for his return in February 1986, almost a year and a half after he had been forced to leave because of AIDS. But first he had to agree to a set of restrictions the principal had devised. In the cafeteria he would use paper plates and plastic utensils that could be thrown away. He would also use a separate water fountain and even a private toilet. And he would not take gym, in case he got cut and infected his classmates by accident.

At last the big day arrived. Escorted by an old friend of the family, Ryan rode to Western High, where hundreds of reporters and TV cameramen had gathered. When one of them asked Ryan how he felt, he said, "I'm real happy."

As things turned out, his happiness was short-lived, for he stayed in school less than a day. The Concerned Citizens and Parents group had carried out their threat to sue if Ryan was allowed to come back, and a judge had issued a restraining order. Ryan would have to remain at home until the case was decided.

While he waited, Ryan and his family had to endure a new wave of rumors about him. The *Kokomo Tribune* published a letter from an anonymous teenager. "Would you want your little brother, sister, cousins, or friends' siblings to be with a young man who constantly threatens to bite, scratch, or spit on children if things aren't done 'his way'?" the letter writer asked.

On Easter Sunday, when everyone in his church traditionally reached out to shake hands with those around them, no one wanted to shake Ryan's hand. Many of his friends stood by Ryan, but other kids drove past his house shouting, "Ryan White's a fag," and throwing beer cans and garbage on the front lawn.

Someone even shot a bullet hole in their front window while the family was away.

Tired and broke, Ryan's mother was tempted to give up the fight, but Ryan and his lawyer pressed on. The lawyer requested that the Concerned Citizens' case be transferred to another county, where Ryan was more likely to get a fair hearing. The request was granted, and a judge in the town of Frankfort dissolved the restraining order. Ryan could go back to Western after all.

Ryan had won, but in many ways it turned out to be a hollow victory. None of the kids wanted to sit next to him or work with him on class projects. In the fall he started coughing again and missed more school when he had to be hospitalized. Tutors helped him to catch up, but soon after he returned to his classes, someone broke into his locker. Whoever it was scrawled graffiti on the walls and wrote "Faggot" and "Queer" all over some folders he had left on the shelf.

At last Ryan had had enough. His mother had wanted to move away from Kokomo for a long time, and now Ryan said he was ready to go, too. With money they had gotten for a TV movie about Ryan, his mother put a down payment on a new house in the small town of Cicero, half an hour south of Kokomo.

The high school Ryan would be attending launched an AIDS-education effort in preparation for his arrival, and there was no trouble on his first day of school in September. Several kids called out, "Hey, Ryan, sit with me!" when he walked into his classrooms, and the school janitor handed him a poem he'd written:

We are sorry for your fight
But for every day that you are here
We can see a little light.

Meanwhile, Ryan had become an even bigger celebrity because of his troubles in Kokomo and the courage he had displayed in battling both hemophilia and AIDS. Whenever they could, he and his family traveled to New York and Los Angeles, where Ryan appeared on TV talk shows and participated in fund-raising events for AIDS research and treatment.

In the spring of 1988, Ryan was invited to speak at a session of the President's Commission on AIDS in Washington, D.C. Nervous and unsure of what to say, he prepared his remarks with the help of his high school English teacher. After telling the commissioners in simple, direct terms what had happened to him in Kokomo, he concluded by saying: "I'm a normal happy teenager again . . . because the students at Hamilton Heights High School listened to the facts, educated their parents and themselves, and believed in me."

During the next year and a half, Ryan enjoyed watching the filming of the TV movie about his life, speaking on behalf of AIDS sufferers, and taking part in as many activities as he could at Hamilton High. Steady doses of AZT helped to keep him healthy. Then, in the fall of 1989, he got sick again. He felt cold all the time, his cough grew worse, and on lots of days he was too tired to go to school.

He rallied, though, and felt strong enough in the spring of 1990 to fly to Los Angeles. There he presented a public-service award to former President Reagan and had his picture taken with Reagan and his wife, Nancy. But he fell ill again during the party that followed and was flown back to Indianapolis that night. As soon as the plane landed, he was rushed to the hospital, where he told his doctor, "I'm so tired of fighting this thing."

Ryan lay unconscious in the hospital for a week, his breathing supported by a ventilator. At last his heart gave out, and he died early in the morning of April 8, 1990. It was Palm Sunday.

THE RYAN WHITE ACT

Thousands paid tribute to Ryan in the days after his death, among them President George Bush. He said, "Ryan has helped us understand the truth about AIDS, and he's shown all of us the strength and bravery of the human heart."

Former President Reagan issued a statement also.

"We owe it to Ryan to make sure that the fear and ig-
norance that chased him from his home and school
will be eliminated," Reagan said. "We owe it to Ryan to
be compassionate, caring, and tolerant toward those
with AIDS, their families and friends."

Would Ryan White have inspired this kind of sympathy if he'd been infected with AIDS through a sexual
act or a drug injection? Judging by President Reagan's
silence during the early years of the epidemic, it's extremely doubtful. But the nation's admiration for Ryan
led Congress to pass a bill that benefited all sufferers
from AIDS, no matter how they had acquired the
disease.

Enacted in August 1990, just four months after his
death, the Ryan White Comprehensive AIDS Resources
Act authorized the expenditure of $4.5 billion over the
next five years to those U.S. communities that had been
hit the hardest by the epidemic. The money would help
public and private agencies in these communities to
provide a full range of AIDS services, from educational
programs for teenagers to hospice care for terminally
ill patients.

The Ryan White Act signaled a new readiness on
the part of the federal government to join in the battle
against AIDS. It also served as a fitting memorial to
the Indiana boy who had bravely fought off both the
disease and the ostracism for more than five years.

Unfortunately, the Act did not mark any lessening in the rate of infection. Hundreds of new AIDS cases were diagnosed each week, and among them were some of the world's most creative individuals.

CHAPTER SIXTEEN

LOSSES AND MEMORIALS

As the 1980s came to an end and the 1990s began, it seemed as if hardly a week went by without word of another well-known person who had succumbed to AIDS. The arts were hit especially hard.

In the performing arts, the disease claimed the lives of the Russian ballet dancer Rudolph Nureyev, the flamboyant pianist Liberace, and actor Anthony Perkins, best known for his role in the movie *Psycho*.

Other casualties in the arts included photographer Robert Mapplethorpe; journalist Randy Shilts, who compiled the first—and as of this writing the only—comprehensive history of AIDS, *And the Band Played On*; and Howard Ashman, who wrote the Oscar-winning lyrics for *Beauty and the Beast* and *The Little Mermaid*.

The disease reached its deadly arm into the sports

field also. Beloved basketball star Magic Johnson stunned his fans in 1991 when he announced he was retiring from the game because he had become infected with the AIDS virus. He said it was the result of his having had promiscuous sex with women, some of them prostitutes.

The following year, Olympic tennis star Arthur Ashe revealed he had contracted AIDS from transfusions administered during a heart operation before the nation's blood supply was screened for HIV. Ashe died nine months later, in early 1993.

Some of these celebrities, like Rudolph Nureyev, tried to keep their illness and its cause a secret to the end. Many had good reasons for doing so. Anthony Perkins's widow said her husband, a bisexual who had had affairs with men, feared that no movie or TV producers would hire him if they knew he was HIV-positive.

Others, like Magic Johnson and Arthur Ashe, took the opposite tack. By announcing their conditions openly, they hoped they might be a force for good in educating the public about the disease. Magic Johnson in particular wanted to warn his young fans of the risks they were taking if they engaged in unprotected sex with multiple partners. At a press conference he admitted he had been naive about the chances of getting AIDS and added, "Here I am saying it can happen to anybody, even me, Magic Johnson."

Whether they went public or kept silent meant little, however, when compared with the losses the world suffered from the illness and death of these celebrities. And they were only the most obvious examples; many other equally talented if less-well-known individuals were lost to the epidemic. The majority died in their prime years, between thirty and fifty. Who knows what books they might have written, what movies they might have made, what music they might have composed, what sports records they might have broken, if their lives had not been cut short by AIDS.

A scientist among them might even have found a vaccine for the disease.

REMEMBERING THE DEAD

As more and more people throughout the world died of AIDS, the grieving survivors felt a strong need to show they had not been forgotten.

The memorials took many different forms. Starting in 1989, Visual AIDS, a nonprofit group of arts professionals, organized "A Day Without Art" and "A Night Without Light." Dedicated to those living with AIDS as well as those who had died, the event was held on December 1, which the World Health Organization of the United Nations had designated as "AIDS Awareness Day."

By 1993, more than 5,300 cultural institutions

around the world were taking part in the commemoration, a thousand more than the year before. On December 1, museums and galleries removed paintings from their walls and draped sculptures in black shrouds to remind visitors of the losses the arts had suffered from AIDS. Between 7:45 and 8:00 that night, television screens went blank for sixty seconds and the floodlights on monuments, bridges, and public buildings were shut off in cities large and small. By order of President Bill Clinton, the lights that illuminated the White House were darkened for the first time.

A more personal way people could demonstrate their concern for AIDS victims was to pin on their clothing a small piece of red ribbon folded over in the middle. The idea for the ribbons came from Visual AIDS, the same organization that promoted "A Day Without Art." It was inspired by the yellow ribbons that thousands of Americans wore in the spring of 1991 to show their support for the soldiers fighting in the Gulf War. The members of Visual AIDS thought: Why not have a similar ribbon to honor those battling AIDS?

The red ribbons were first worn by residents of SoHo, the downtown artists' district in New York City. Soon they appeared on many of the stars who participated in the nationally televised Oscar, Emmy, and MTV awards ceremonies. After that, it wasn't long before the ribbons could be seen on coat lapels, blouses, shirts, and dresses from New York to Chicago to Los Angeles—a symbol of their wearers' commitment to the struggle against AIDS.

THE AIDS MEMORIAL QUILT

The largest, most impressive, and many would say the most moving AIDS memorial is the Quilt. It was conceived in 1985 by Cleve Jones, a gay-rights activist in San Francisco who had lost many friends and loved ones to the disease. But he drew on an American quilt-making tradition that dates back to colonial times.

The early settlers often stitched records of family births, marriages, and deaths into the squares of their quilts. In much the same way, each panel in the AIDS Memorial Quilt is a tribute to someone who has been lost to the disease. Created by those who remember them, the panels are an expression of the love their makers felt for friends, husbands, wives, lovers—or children.

As of February 1995, there were 29,000 individual three-by-six-foot panels in the Quilt, and more are constantly being added. When the entire Quilt was displayed in Washington in 1992, it covered the equivalent of thirteen football fields. Between such large displays, sections of the Quilt are shown in smaller exhibits around the county. In 1994 alone, portions of it were displayed in more than 1,600 different locations, often as part of AIDS Awareness programs.

By the beginning of 1995, it was estimated that at least 5 million men, women, and children had viewed parts of the AIDS Memorial Quilt. As they read the testimonies of love and loss inscribed on its panels, they were reminded not only of all those who had died, but of the urgent need to find some means of ending the epidemic. Unfortunately, there were no indications in the early months of 1995 that such a scientific breakthrough was likely anytime soon. In fact, the latest reports from the research front were almost all discouraging.

CHAPTER SEVENTEEN

NO END IN SIGHT

In the early 1990s, scientists involved in AIDS research were hopeful of making rapid progress in their struggle against the disease.

They based their optimism on two recent studies. One suggested that giving AZT to HIV-infected people whose T-cell counts were below 500, but who were otherwise healthy, could postpone any further decline in their immune systems for many years. The other seemed to show that a combination of AZT with two other antiviral drugs thwarted HIV's ability to develop resistance to the drugs when they were administered singly.

But by 1994, doubts had been raised about the conclusions of both studies. Longer-term investigations had found that the beneficial effects of AZT in people with T-cell counts below 500 often wore off after a year or two, and that the drug's early application did not necessarily result in longer lives. At the same time, the experiments with the use of three drugs against the virus turned out to have serious flaws.

Even more discouraging was the news about several experimental AIDS vaccines that had once looked promising. The vaccines were made from components of HIV that scientists had grown in laboratories. Their creators hoped the vaccines would trick the immune system into generating protective antibodies, and indeed they did so when injected into human volunteers. Moreover, the antibodies appeared to destroy strains of laboratory-grown HIV.

Expectantly, the scientists tested the antibodies against viruses isolated from humans, only to have their hopes frustrated. The antibodies had no effect whatsoever on that type of HIV. Dr. David Ho, Director of the Aaron Diamond AIDS Research Center in New York, said researchers would simply have to begin again, making vaccines from viruses isolated from AIDS patients. "It's not any harder, " he said. "It's just that we have to start over."

Assuming a vaccine is developed, a big question will remain: Can any single vaccine be effective against the hundreds of different forms the AIDS virus may take? Only time, and much further experimentation, can provide the answer to that.

A quicker path to a cure may be found by studying why some individuals who are HIV-positive remain healthy and vigorous for a dozen or more years after being infected. On average, it takes less than ten years for an infected person to be attacked by one of the life-threatening diseases that signal full-blown AIDS.

Researchers have discovered that long-term survivors, as they are called, have high levels of infection-fighting white blood cells known as CD8 cells. These cells secrete a protein that keeps the AIDS virus from reproducing. The researchers are trying to find ways to increase the production of this vital protein in the cells of others who are HIV-infected. If they succeed, these people, too, may enjoy a lifespan comparable to that of the long-term survivors.

AROUND THE WORLD

In the meantime, the HIV infection rate has been rising higher in every corner of the world. According to a 1994 estimate made by the World Health Organization, 19.5 million people throughout the world had contracted HIV since the epidemic began, and more than 4.5 million had developed AIDS. Brazil ranked second only to the United States in the number of reported AIDS cases. Sexual promiscuity by bisexual men and limited prevention efforts have fueled the spread of the epidemic in this large South American country.

The nations of southeast Asia have also been hit hard, especially Thailand. In this country where prostitution flourishes, health officials estimate that as much as five percent of the population is infected with the AIDS virus. (This compares with an infection rate in the United States of less than one percent.) Among Thai prostitutes—many of whom are teenage girls brought to cities from country villages—the rate of infection can be as high as seventy-five percent.

Suffering the most are the impoverished nations of central Africa, where the AIDS epidemic started and where it continues to ravage the population. In central Africa, AIDS is transmitted primarily through heterosexual sex. Many men in this region have two or more wives, which helps to spread the disease if the men become infected with the virus. There is little in the way of treatment available to those who fall ill. Hospitals are few and far between and lack clean bedding, let alone expensive drugs like AZT.

As a result, many children in countries like Uganda and Zaire have lost both parents to AIDS. In one rural district of Uganda, a 1991 census revealed that one child in four was an orphan. Thirteen-year-old Julius Keeya Kintu is typical of these orphaned children. He and his six younger brothers and sisters are trying to scrape out a living from the two hilly acres their parents left them.

"My father taught me how to plant, and my mother, she taught me discipline," Julius told a reporter from *The New York Times.* "When I am older, I want to be a doctor. I see so many people who are sick and they die before they even get to the hospital."

With the HIV infection rate rising steadily throughout the world and no cure for AIDS in sight, increased emphasis has been put on AIDS education and other preventive measures. They seem the only sure means of slowing, if not halting, the spread of the disease. But many of these measures have stirred up controversies when put into practice.

NEEDLE EXCHANGE PROGRAMS

One such controversy surrounded needle exchange programs for addicts who inject drugs. Since most addicts acquire the AIDS virus by sharing contaminated needles and syringes, health officials in New York, San Francisco, and other cities devised experimental programs whereby addicts could exchange their used, dirty needles for clean ones.

Inner-city clergymen and other leaders immediately denounced the needle exchange programs. They charged that it implied government acceptance of drug abuse. They also feared it would encourage more people to inject illegal drugs by making the procedure seem safer.

An in-depth study of the programs was conducted by the Centers for Disease Control. The study showed that addicts who participated in such programs were less likely to develop viral diseases such as hepatitis B that are spread through needles. This seemed to indicate that they would be less likely to contract HIV also. At the same time, the study found no evidence that clean-needle programs increased the level of drug use in a community.

Many of those who had opposed the needle exchanges were still not convinced. They argued that the only sure way to halt the spread of AIDS among addicts was to find medical, economic, and political solutions to the entire drug problem.

Health officials are agreed that would be the best long-term policy. Meanwhile, though, they have to deal with the short-term reality that addicts, their sexual partners, and their children now account for more than a third of all the reported AIDS cases in the United States. The HIV infection rate has fallen among gay men, but it continues to rise rapidly in the addict population.

Given that fact, the officials weren't about to abandon needle exchange programs. If anything, they hoped to expand them, so that more drug abusers could be protected against infection by HIV.

CONDOMS, PRO AND CON

A similar controversy arose concerning the distribution of latex condoms to sexually active teenagers in New York City high schools.

Only about three percent of the nation's teenagers live in New York, but by 1992 they accounted for twenty percent of all reported cases of adolescent AIDS in the United States. In an attempt to reduce this high percentage, the New York City Board of Education authorized the distribution of condoms in all of the city's 126 high schools. Students could obtain the condoms from trained staff in their schools' health resource rooms. They did not have to have their parents' consent.

The Roman Catholic Church and Orthodox Jewish organizations expressed their firm opposition to the plan. Like those who were against giving clean needles to drug abusers, the clergy claimed that making condoms available to teenagers would encourage sexual promiscuity. In no uncertain terms, the clergy said that abstinence was the only sure way to prevent sexual transmission of the AIDS virus, and that it and it alone should be the focus of any AIDS education efforts.

A group of conservative parents filed a lawsuit against the Board of Education, charging that the condom distribution plan violated their right to raise their children as they saw fit. A state court agreed with the parents, and the plan was modified accordingly. Now parents would be notified before the plan was put into effect, and would have the final say as to whether or not their children participated in it.

Peace was restored for the moment as far as the condom distribution plan was concerned. But the underlying problem of teenagers and the AIDS virus remained in place—not just in New York City but throughout the country. According to a 1993 survey conducted by health experts, young people are experimenting with sex at ever-earlier ages. More than a third of fifteen-year-old boys reported that they had had sexual intercourse, as did twenty-seven percent of fifteen-year-old girls. In the city of Cleveland, the average age for first sexual intercourse is twelve and a half.

Along with all of these early experiences goes the risk of getting a sexually transmitted disease like AIDS. Young people are well aware of this possibility. In a poll conducted for *Newsweek* magazine in 1994, fear of contracting the AIDS virus ranked first among the concerns of youths between nine and seventeen. They had good reason to be fearful. One fifth of all AIDS patients are under thirty, and since the incubation period for the disease can be eight years or more, most of them were probably infected in their teenage years.

Knowing the dangers, how can young people deal

with their sexual impulses in the age of AIDS? Postponing sex is still the safest course to follow, and many youth organizations actively promote abstinence today. Role-playing workshops in Georgia, California, and other states give young people the skills to fend off sexual advances and say no to early intercourse. Teenage girls in Baltimore are joining virgin clubs, and public service billboards along Maryland highways deliver messages like "Abstinence Makes the Heart Grow Fonder" and "Virginity Is *Not* a Dirty Word."

But what about those young people who, due to peer pressure or their own drives, *are* having sex? Should they simply be left to their own devices and not be given in-depth sex education, or health aids like condoms with which they can protect themselves?

Following in the footsteps of C. Everett Koop, Dr. M. Joycelyn Elders, the first Surgeon General in the Clinton administration, came out in favor of a realistic approach to the problem. In an interview published in *The New York Times Magazine* in 1994, Dr. Elders said: "All we have to do is look at the numbers of young people getting pregnant, getting AIDS, getting sexually transmitted diseases. . . . People realize that we all support the moral view, but we know that an awful lot of our children are not being abstinent. . . . Since we can't legislate morals, we have to teach them how to take care of themselves."

When asked how she felt about the label "condom queen," which had been pinned on her by conservative lobbying organizations opposed to her policies, Dr. Elders said: "Listen, coming from them, it doesn't bother me. If I could be the 'condom queen' and get every young person who is engaged in sex to use a condom in the United States, I would wear a crown on my head with a condom on it! I would!"

Dr. Elders's outspoken and often controversial opinions helped lead to her abrupt resignation as surgeon general in December 1994. But the need remains for a realistic approach to sex education, one that combines lessons in how to resist social and peer pressure with the distribution of condoms when necessary. Agreement on such an approach isn't likely to be reached anytime soon, however, given the strong feelings of those on both sides of the issue.

Meanwhile, one thing is certain. The AIDS epidemic has forced the American public to confront aspects of sexuality and drug addiction that had not been discussed openly before. This confrontation has made some people extremely uncomfortable, while others have hailed it as a step toward greater understanding and tolerance. Whatever one's attitude, the discussion is sure to continue in the future, no matter what course the AIDS epidemic may take.

* * *

And that's as far as the story of AIDS can be taken, in the early months of 1995. Unlike the bubonic plague, AIDS has by no means been brought under control. Nor has another Edward Jenner come forth with the equivalent of a smallpox vaccine that will halt the spread of the AIDS virus and eventually wipe it out. At this point, the best one can hope for is that scientists will gradually unlock more of the virus's secrets and find ways to outsmart it so that those suffering from the disease can lead longer, healthier lives. If that goal can be achieved, the next generation may be spared the devastating losses that this generation has suffered.

In the meantime, sad to say, AIDS is not the only puzzling and frightening new disease that has appeared on the scene.

AFTERWORD

THE ENEMY IS ALIVE AND WELL

In May 1993, an athletic-looking young Navajo could barely breathe when he stumbled into the Indian Medical Center in Gallup, New Mexico. Doctors immediately X-rayed his chest and saw that his lungs were drowning in fluid. They did everything they could to save him, but it was too late. Within hours the husky nineteen-year-old man died.

He was one of more than twenty Navajos, most of them young, who came down with a mysterious new disease in the spring of 1993. All of them lived on the Navajo Reservation that stretches across the northeast corner of Arizona into New Mexico and Utah.

The disease began with flulike symptoms—muscle aches, coughing, and fever. But less than forty-eight hours later its victims were fighting for breath as their lungs filled with fluid. If they weren't given antibodies or put on a mechanical ventilator within six hours after the breathing problems started, death came quickly, as it did to the young Navajo man.

Doctors in the region had no idea what was causing the outbreak and called on the Centers for Disease Control and Prevention in Atlanta for help. Scientists from the CDC soon arrived on the scene. They joined forces with local health officials and traditional Navajo healers to discover how the victims were exposed to the disease and try to find a way to bring the epidemic under control.

The scientists first tested tissue samples from the victims for the germs that cause bubonic plague and other bacterial diseases. After these tests failed to yield any results, the scientists searched the tissues for such common viruses as influenza and chicken pox. Again they came up with nothing.

At this point, the Navajo healers suggested that the region's rodent population might be involved in transmitting the disease. The mild, wet winter had kept food supplies abundant and made the ground soft and easy to burrow into. As the healers had traveled about the reservation, they had noticed many more deer mice than usual.

Picking up on the healers' suggestion, the CDC scientists trapped more than eight hundred mice throughout the 26,000-square-mile reservation. Tests showed that thirty percent of the mice had antibodies to an organism called hantavirus in their systems.

This finding puzzled the scientists. The hantavirus, which, like the bubonic plague, is carried by rodents, strikes hundreds of thousands of people in Asia each year. It had rarely been seen in North America, however. In addition, the virus in Asia causes a flulike illness that can lead to internal bleeding, kidney failure, and often death. But it does not normally attack the lungs.

The scientists wondered if the hantavirus might have assumed a deadly new form in the American Southwest. They proceeded to test the tissues of nine human sufferers of the mysterious disease, and sure enough—they found antibodies to the hantavirus in six of them. This indicated that the Navajo healers were right in thinking the virus was transmitted by infected rodents.

Health officials announced the scientists' findings and warned people in the region to avoid all contact with rodents, their droppings, and their burrows. The officials speculated that the virus was spread through the air on dust particles that had been contaminated by the urine and feces of sick rodents. People became infected when they inhaled the particles. There was no evidence that the disease was transmitted person to person, nor that it was insect-borne.

By November 1993, forty-five cases of what was

now called hantavirus pulmonary syndrome had been reported in the western United States, and twenty-seven of the victims had died. A number of the cases involved young adults who had become infected while on camping trips in wilderness areas.

Fortunately, the large-scale epidemic that some scientists had feared did not develop. But the CDC continued to keep a close watch on this devastating illness for which there is, as yet, no preventive vaccine.

Meanwhile, an even more alarming situation had developed in the health field. A number of disease-causing bacteria that were thought to be under control suddenly began to resist treatment.

THE FAILURE OF ANTIBIOTICS

The fifty-seven-year-old kidney patient had been treated with one antibiotic drug after another at the Veterans Affairs Medical Center in Washington, D.C. No matter what combination of tablets and capsules the man was given, nothing worked. For a short time his blood would test clean, but after a few days it would be swarming again with the streptococcus bacteria that were slowly poisoning his red blood cells. Late in 1993, the man finally died from a massive infection of the blood and heart.

What had gone wrong? Why hadn't penicillin or ampicillin or one of the other "wonder drugs" discovered during the twentieth century been able to cure the man's illness and save his life?

Because disease bacteria have found ways to outwit the drugs. "Ever since 1928, when Alexander Fleming discovered penicillin, man and microbe have been in a footrace," Dr. Richard Wenzel of the University of Iowa told a *Newsweek* magazine reporter in 1994. "Right now the microorganisms are winning. They're so much older than we are . . . and wiser."

The wisdom of disease bacteria lies in the fact that at least some of them can develop resistance to antibiotics. For example, if a patient suffering from a bacterial disease is given a massive dose of penicillin, most of the infection-causing bacteria in his or her system will be killed. But perhaps a few of the bacteria have different genes from the others—different in that they are resistant to the drug and thus able to survive. These resistant bacteria will be the only ones left to reproduce. Bacteria have an extremely high rate of reproduction, so within a short while there will be trillions of them that are resistant to penicillin.

Other antibiotics, given in conjunction with penicillin or by themselves, may succeed in killing this new type of resistant bacteria. But in time still newer varieties are bound to emerge against which none of the available antibiotics are effective. That's what happened in the case of the patient who died of blood poisoning at the Washington, D.C., Medical Center.

In the past few years, strains of pneumococcus, a bacterium that can cause ear infections and pneumonia, have become resistant to penicillin and four other antibiotics. And more than twenty percent of the microbes responsible for tuberculosis no longer respond to treatment with antibiotics. This is one of the reasons tuberculosis, an often-fatal lung disease that scientists thought had been controlled, has reappeared with a vengeance in large cities like New York, especially among people with lowered immune responses.

If this trend continues, it's conceivable that a new plague as devastating as the Black Death could sweep the world. What steps can be taken to prevent such a catastrophe from occurring?

To start with, doctors can stop prescribing antibiotics for viral infections, such as the common cold, against which they are useless. This only speeds up the process that kills the weaker microbes in the patient's system while letting resistant strains survive and multiply.

Farmers can stop overdosing their cattle and chickens with penicillin and tetracycline. True, these antibiotics treat and prevent infection and make the animals grow faster from each pound of feed they consume. Resistant bacteria strains remain in the animals' tissues, however, and they may spread to humans through raw or undercooked meat.

On the research front, scientists are searching for new drugs to replace those that have proved ineffective. They are also trying to discover how the microbes outwit existing antibiotics so that they can construct new drugs that will take advantage of the microbes' weaknesses. But government and corporate money for basic research is in short supply in the United States and other countries, so it may be some time before the scientists have any breakthroughs to report.

Meanwhile, people everywhere must learn to accept the fact that the disease-causing bacteria and viruses that have always tormented humans aren't about to give up and go away. We may appear at times to have won the battle against them. We may even be tempted to proclaim, as some scientists did in the 1970s, that infectious disease will soon be conquered once and for all. Then a frightening new disease like AIDS comes along and shocks us out of our complacency.

When such a disease develops into a raging epidemic, it's easy to sink into despair, as many did in the face of the bubonic plague, smallpox, and more recently AIDS. It's also easy to blame our miseries on scapegoats—the Jews of Germany at the time of the Black Death, homosexual men in the age of AIDS.

Every major plague that has afflicted the world seems to have brought out the best as well as the worst in people. There have always been doctors, clergy, friends, and neighbors who cared for the victims, often at risk to their own lives. And there have been others who refused all contact with the sufferers, even going so far as to wall them up in their own homes.

Judging from what has happened in the past, these behavior patterns are likely to be repeated in the future should some terrible new plague strike the world. They needn't, though, if we remain alert to each new disease that appears on the scene, and quickly mobilize all our scientific and medical resources in a struggle against it.

Above all, we should remember our common humanity. A child orphaned by AIDS in Africa or a teenage prostitute fighting the virus in Thailand may not seem to have any connection to us. But in today's world, where one can fly to any continent within a matter of hours, they do.

It took centuries for smallpox to reach the natives of North and South America from Europe. Things are very different now. Whether a new disease arises in central Africa, as AIDS apparently did, or in the deserts of the American Southwest, like the pulmonary hantavirus, it may be only a matter of days or weeks before it makes the journey from one continent to another.

Given this undeniable fact, no new disease can remain a problem for only one group, nation, or even continent. Finding ways to treat and cure it soon becomes the concern of everyone on the planet.

SOURCE NOTES AND BIBLIOGRAPHY

So many books, magazine articles, and newspaper reports were part of the research for *When Plague Strikes* that it would be virtually impossible to list them all. Here I'll single out those that contributed significantly to the planning and writing of the book.

OVERALL

Four books stimulated my thinking when I was deciding how to treat the subject of plagues in history. They were:

Plagues and Peoples by William H. McNeill (New York: Doubleday, 1977). This fascinating book describes the decisive role that disease has played in the historical development of the human race. From it I gained a much clearer notion of how plagues like the Black Death could travel from one continent to another.

The Doctor in History by Howard W. Haggard (New York: Dorset Press, 1989). A history of medicine and its practitioners from prehistoric times to the early years of the twentieth century. While not up-to-date, it contains valuable material on early physicians such as Hippocrates and Galen.

Disease and History by Frederick F. Cartwright, in collaboration with Michael D. Boddiss (New York: Dorset Press, 1991). Includes accounts of many epidemics, from the Biblical plagues in ancient Egypt to recent worldwide problems with environmental pollution and the ills that it causes. It was in this book that I first read about the Plague of Athens.

Rats, Lice, and History: The Biography of a Bacillus by Hans Zinsser (Boston: The Atlantic Monthly Press/Little, Brown and Company, 1934). This "biography" of the bacillus that causes typhus conveys the persistence and dedication that are a vital part of all scientific investigations.

REFERENCES FOR SPECIFIC SECTIONS
Prologue: The Plague of Athens

The quotations from Thucydides in the Prologue come from his *History of the Peloponnesian War*, translated by Rex Warner with an introduction and notes by M. I. Finley (London and New York: Penguin Books, 1954, 1972).

The Black Death

Two general histories of the epidemic were most helpful when I was researching this section:

The Black Death: Natural and Human Disaster in Medieval Europe by Robert S. Gottfried (New York: The Free Press/A Division of Macmillan Publishing Co., Inc., 1983).

The Black Death by Philip Ziegler (New York: Harper & Row, Publishers, 1971).

Gottfried is especially good on the economic and environmental factors that helped to spread the plague, and the tremendous social changes that occurred in its wake. Ziegler's book is filled with specific details and presents a vivid picture of the Flagellants and the persecution of the Jews.

Other Sources (in the order that the material they relate to appears in the text)

"How a Mysterious Disease Laid Low Europe's Masses," an article by Charles L. Mee, Jr., (*Smithsonian*, February 1990), includes a dramatic account of the plague's transmission by rats and fleas that helped me to better understand this complicated process.

The quotations from *The Decameron* by Giovanni Boccaccio in Chapter One are from the edition translated with an introduction by G. H. McWilliam (London and New York: Penguin Books, 1972).

The Oxford Dictionary of Nursery Rhymes, edited by Iona and Peter Opie (London: Oxford University Press, 1951), provided the text of the earliest published version of "Ring-a-ring o' roses." However, the Opies do not subscribe to the theory that this rhyme was first chanted during the years of the Black Death. I came across that theory in the Mee article and several other sources.

A Distant Mirror: The Calamitous 14th Century by Barbara Tuchman (New York: Ballantine Books, 1979) contains a chapter on the Black Death from which I drew additional information about antisemitism in Germany at the time of the epidemic.

Facts about the return of the bubonic plague in the seventeenth century came primarily from *The London Encyclopedia*, edited by Ben Weinreb and Christopher Hibbert (Bethesda,

Md.: Adler & Adler Publishers, Inc., 1986; London: Macmillan London, 1983).

The Diary of Samuel Pepys: Selections, edited by O. F. Morshead, illustrated by Ernest H. Shepard (Gloucester, Mass.: Peter Smith, 1973) was the source for the extract from Pepys's diary that appears in Chapter Six.

Reports by John F. Burns and Philip M. Boffey in *The New York Times*, September–November 1994, provided information on the outbreak of pneumonic plague in India.

Smallpox

The two comprehensive histories of the disease that I referred to throughout this section were:

Princes and Peasants: Smallpox in History by Donald R. Hopkins (Chicago and London: The University of Chicago Press, 1983)

The Invisible Fire by Joel N. Shurkin (New York: G. P. Putnam's Sons, 1979).

Hopkins's book is chock-full of information about the myths that grew up around smallpox in ancient China and India, and the social history of the disease in later centuries. Shurkin's book offers a thorough and dramatic account of the final eradication of smallpox in the 1960s and 1970s.

Other Sources

The Buried Mirror: Reflections on Spain and the New World by Carlos Fuentes (Boston: Houghton Mifflin Company, 1992). This scholarly work stimulated my thinking about the destructive impact Spanish forces had on the civilizations of the Americas.

Jared Diamond's provocative article "The Arrow of Disease" (*Discover Magazine*, October 1992) brought home to me the key role disease played in the conquest of the Aztecs and the Incas.

The Life of Mary Wortley Montagu by Robert Halsbrand (London: Oxford University Press, 1958) helped me to get a clearer picture of this remarkable woman and her many accomplishments.

The Americans: The Colonial Experience by Daniel J. Boorstin (New York: Vintage Books/A Division of Random House, 1958) provided enlightening details about Cotton Mather's activities in support of inoculation during the Boston smallpox epidemic of 1721.

Jenner's Smallpox Vaccine by Derrick Baxby (London: Heinemann, 1981) expanded my knowledge of the British doctor and scientist's pathbreaking work.

Letters and Notes on the Manners, Customs, and Conditions of North American Indians by George Catlin (Minneapolis: Ross and Haines, Inc., 1965) gave me an excellent overview, laced with firsthand impressions, of the smallpox epidemics that struck the Indians of the upper Midwest in the 1820s and 1830s.

The Village Indians of the Upper Missouri: The Mandans, Hidatsas, and Arikaras by Roy W. Meyer (Lincoln, Neb., and London: University of Nebraska Press, 1977) filled out Catlin's account of what happened when smallpox virtually wiped out the Mandan tribe in 1837.

For information on the continuing debate about what to do with the two remaining stocks of smallpox virus, I relied on reports published in *The New York Times, Newsweek,* and other periodicals in 1993 , 1994, and 1995.

AIDS

To my knowledge, only one full-scale history of the AIDS epidemic has been written thus far. It is Randy Shilts's monumental work *And the Band Played On: Politics, People, and the AIDS Epidemic* (New York: St. Martin's Press, 1987), and I leaned on it heavily in tracing the course of the epidemic from the late 1970s until 1987.

Other Sources: Books

AIDS Today, Tomorrow: An Introduction to the HIV Epidemic in America by Robert Searles Walker (Atlantic Highlands, N.J., and London: Humanities Press International, Inc., 1991). A biology professor from San Antonio, Texas, discusses the social and political issues generated by the AIDS crisis, and carries the chronicle forward to 1990. His book reveals the impact the disease has had in smaller cities and towns far from such centers as New York and San Francisco.

The Social Impact of AIDS in the United States, edited by Albert R. Jonsen and Jeff Stryker for the National Research Council (Washington, D.C.: National Academy Press, 1993). This report of a government panel explores how the disease has affected the policies and practices of the country's major scientific, medical, and religious institutions. I found especially illuminating the coverage of AIDS activists and their fight to get new drugs tested and approved.

100 Questions and Answers About AIDS: What You Need to Know Now by Michael Thomas Ford (New York: Beech Tree Paperbacks, 1993). Written for teenagers, and featuring interviews with four young people who are living with AIDS, this book raises the questions most often asked about the disease and provides solid, honest answers. A useful Resource Guide is included.

Conduct Unbecoming: Gays and Lesbians in the U.S. Military by Randy Shilts (New York: St. Martin's Press, 1993). Here I located a clear account of the military's policies toward recruits and service personnel who test positive for the AIDS virus.

Ryan White: My Own Story by Ryan White and Ann Marie Cunningham (New York: Dial Books, 1991). Completed shortly before his death, this first-person account captures the courage and spirit of the Indiana teenager who battled AIDS and won the nation's admiration.

My Life by Earvin "Magic" Johnson with William Novak (New York: Random House, Inc., 1992). A no-holds-barred account of the basketball star's life, written after he tested positive for the AIDS virus.

Other Sources: Articles

"A Modern-Day Plague" by Jonathan E. Kaplan (*Natural History*, February 1986) and "The Natural History of AIDS" by Matthew Allen Gonda (*Natural History*, May 1986) helped me to understand how the AIDS virus goes about its deadly work.

The Harvard AIDS Letter, November/December 1993, contained an unaccredited article that provided me with information on Cleve Jones and the beginnings of the AIDS Quilt.

"Whatever Happened to AIDS?" by Jeffrey Schmalz (*The New York Times Magazine*, November 28, 1993) is both a report on the crisis and a harrowing description of the author's ultimately futile struggle against the disease. Schmalz died a few weeks before the article appeared.

"In Search of the Cure for AIDS: A special report from the

frontiers of science" by Robert Sullivan (*Rolling Stone*, April 7, 1994) furnished me with an excellent summary of current AIDS research at the time I was completing this book.

The direct quotations of Dr. M. Joycelyn Elders, U.S. Surgeon General until December of 1994, were taken from "Joycelyn Elders," a profile by Claudia Dreifus (*The New York Times Magazine*, January 30, 1994).

Information on the other main developments in the AIDS crisis from 1987 to 1995 was drawn mainly from journalistic coverage of the epidemic in *The New York Times*, *The Washington Post*, *Newsweek*, *Time*, and other periodicals. The reports of *New York Times* writers Lawrence K. Altman, Jeffrey Schmalz, Gina Kolata, and Natalie Angier were especially useful.

Afterword: The Enemy Is Alive and Well

The facts about the hantavirus outbreak in the American Southwest came from accounts published in *The New York Times*, *Newsweek*, and *The Village Voice* in the summer and fall of 1993.

Material about the failure of certain antibiotics to control specific diseases was taken from reports that appeared in *Newsweek* and *The New York Times* early in 1994.

INDEX